NORTHAMPTONSHIRE

Place Names

NORTHAMPTONSHIRE

Place Names

Anthony Poulton-Smith

AMBERLEY

First published 2010

Amberley Publishing
Cirencester Road, Chalford,
Stroud, Gloucestershire, GL6 8PE

www.amberley-books.com

British Library Cataloguing in Publication Data.
A catalogue record for this book is available from the British Library.

ISBN 978 1 84868 718 9

Typesetting and origination by Amberley Publishing
Printed in Great Britain by the MPG Books Group

Contents

Introduction

For years, the history of England was based on the Roman occupation. In recent years, we have come to realise the influence of the Empire did not completely rewrite British history; indeed, there was already a thriving culture in England well before the birth of Christ. When the Romans left our shores in the fifth century, the arrival of the Anglo-Saxons was thought to herald a time of turmoil, yet they brought the culture and language which forms the basis of modern England. The same is true of our place names: the vast majority of settlement names in Northamptonshire are derived from this Saxon or Old English language. However, the close proximity to the Danelaw region of England has resulted in the influence of the Scandinavian tongues, though very few examples are derived from this tongue. There are also the topographical features, such as rivers and hills, which still have names given to them by the Celts of the pre-Roman era.

Ostensibly, place names are simply descriptions of the location, or its uses and the people who lived there. In the pages that follow, an examination of the origins and meanings of the names in Northamptonshire will reveal all. Not only will we see Saxon and Scandinavian settlements, but Celtic rivers, Roman roads and even Norman French landlords, who have all contributed, to some degree, to the evolution of the names we are otherwise so familiar with.

Not only are the basic names discussed but also districts, hills, streams, fields, roads, lanes, streets and public houses. Road and street names are normally of more recent derivation, named after those who played a significant role in the development of a town, or revealing what existed in the village before the developers moved in. The benefactors who provided housing and employment in the eighteenth and nineteenth centuries are often forgotten, yet their names live on in the name found on the sign at the end of the street and often have a story to tell. Pub names are almost a language of their own. Again, they are not named arbitrarily but are based on the history of the place and can open a new window on the history of our towns and villages.

Defining place names of all varieties can give an insight into history that would otherwise be ignored or even lost. In the ensuing pages, we shall examine 2,000-plus years of Northamptonshire history. While driving around this area, the author was delighted by the quintessentially English place names around the area and so, having already taken a look at *Oxfordshire Place Names, Hampshire Place Names, Gloucestershire Place Names, North Devon Place Names, South Devon Place Names, Dorset Place Names* and *Somerset Place Names*, turned to Northamptonshire. This book is the result of the author's long interest in place names, which has developed over many years, and is the latest in a series that continues to intrigue and surprise.

To all who helped in my research, from the librarians who produced the written word to those who pointed a lost traveller in the right direction, a big thank you.

Chapter 1

Abthorpe–Aynho

ABTHORPE

Listings of this name include Torp in 1086, Abetrop in 1190, and Abbethorp in 1230 and it describes 'Abba's outlying farmstead'. There is no doubt this is a Saxon personal name, however, these forms are not early enough to show if the suffix is Old English *throp* or Old Scandinavian *thorp*. The first element is hardly a clue, for there are innumerable examples of hybrid names, especially in those counties under the influence of both cultures prior to the arrival of the Normans.

Local names include Bucknell Wood, a name from Old English *bucen hyll* and describing 'the hill covered by beech trees'. The name of Charlock Farm also refers to the locality, here pointing to 'the cold streamlet'.

The local pub is the New Inn, a name which is self-explanatory but also tells us there must have been an earlier pub here.

ACHURCH

The origins of this name seem quite clear. Yet examining the earliest listings of Asencircan in 972, Aseyrcan in 992, and Asechirce in 1086, it is clear the name does not simply mean 'a church'. The suffix is undoubtedly the Old English *cirice*, however, the first element is a personal name, either Saxon Asa or Scandinavian Asi; the early records are inconclusive.

Here we also find Thorpe Achurch, which features the element *thorp* or 'outlying farmstead'. Thorpe Waterville is another 'outlying farmstead', this time associated with the family of Ascelin de Waterville in the twelfth century.

ADSTONE

Only two records of note here, as Atenestone in Domesday and, a century later, as Etteneston. Oddly, the later form points to the normally unreliable Domesday being closer to the original in spelling, if not pronunciation, although the suffix has become corrupted. This is the Old English *tun*, not a *stan* or 'stone', giving us 'Aettin's farmstead'.

AILSWORTH

Found as Aegelesuurth in 948, Egleswurthe in 972, and Eglesworde in 1086, this name is undoubtedly from 'Aegels' enclosure'.

Locally, Wildboars Coppice does not point to the animal recently re-introduced to parts of Britain; this is a reference to the Wildbore family, who were important landowners here in the sixteenth and seventeenth centuries.

ALDERTON

A common place name found in several counties around the Midlands, although not always with the same meaning. Recorded in Domesday as Aldritone and in 1186 as Aldrinton, this name comes from a Saxon personal name with Old English *ing* and *tun* giving 'the farmstead of the people or followers of Ealdhere'.

ALDWINCLE

The suffix seen here is Old English *wincel*, an unusual but not unknown element. Here, it follows a personal name and tells us of '(the place at) the river bend associated with a man called Ealda'. It is probably the largest place in the country to have this element in its name. Once there were two separate parishes, Aldwincle St Peter and Aldwincle All Saints, each named after the dedication of the respective churches, although they have now officially merged.

Minor names here include Bradshaw Wood, from *brad haga*, describing 'the broad-hedged enclosure'; Brancey Bridge is from 'Brant's *eg* or dry land in wetland'; and Old Lyveden and New Lyveden share the common origin of 'Leofa's valley'.

This was the birthplace of poet John Dryden (1631-1700), the eldest of fourteen children and a second cousin of Jonathan Swift. He was poet laureate from 1668-86.

ALTHORP

This ancestral home of the Spencer family has a name with an unusual pronunciation. Brought to the attention of the nation at large by its most famous resident, the spelling suggests Althorp but is actually pronounced as Althrop. Listings of the name are found as Olletorp in 1086 and Olethorp in 1208, which is certainly 'Olla's outlying farmstead'.

However, the origin is questionable and explains the apparent contrast in the written and spoken forms. The element is unquestionably either Old English *throp* or Old Scandinavian *thorp*, both with identical meaning and having a common root in the Indo-European language group. As can be seen from these old languages, the verbal form seems to be Old English and the written form Old Scandinavian. This is doubtless the explanation, as Northamptonshire would have been influenced by both cultures and languages. Invariably the verbal form is the correct one; however, it is highly unusual not to find the Scandinavian version in use today.

APETHORPE

Domesday's record of this place name shows just how unreliable the great work can be when it comes to proper names. Compare the 1086 record of Patorp with the modern form and those of Apetorp in 1163 and Appetorp in 1167; today, it would be dismissed as simply typographical and yet this cannot have been the case in the eleventh century. The origin here is Old Scandinavian with the personal name being followed by *thorp* giving 'Api's outlying farmstead'.

Halefield Lodge comes from *halh feld* and describes 'the open land in the nook of land'. Note that while a modern 'field' and the Saxon *feld* were ostensibly the same thing, and clearly one has evolved from the other, both physically and etymologically, the Saxon version was rather different. Forget any idea of neat woven hedges or a strong fence surrounding a crop or pasture. Dismiss any notion of a gate keeping the livestock from wandering. This was simply an area cleared of trees and undergrowth, the debris being pushed to the perimeter to mark out the *feld*.

ARMSTON

Found as Mermeston in 1086, Armeston in 1202, as Ermeston in 1227, and as Armistone in 1232, here is a name which features a Saxon place name and describes 'Earnmund's farmstead'.

Burray Spinney is a corruption of *burh weg* or 'the fortification by the way', while Coney Geer Coppice was once a managed 'rabbit warren'.

ARTHINGWORTH

No shortage of early forms of this name, from 1086 as Arningwode, 1202 as Erningwrth, 1220 as Arningwrth, and 1274 as Arthingworth, this can be seen to have come from the Old English. Here, a personal name has been followed by *inga* and *worth* giving 'the enclosure of the people or followers of Earna'. When speaking of a *worth* in Saxon times, the image that comes to mind is one of a defensive structure intended to keep out invaders. In reality, it was a fence or palings designed to keep the livestock safe overnight.

ASHBY ST LEDGERS

One of the most common place names in that part of the country, where there was Scandinavian influence, which always describes 'the village of or near the ash trees'. Such common names are often found with a second element to make it stand out and to avoid confusion. At the time of Domesday, there was no distinction, simply listed as Ascebi, yet by 1248, we find Esseby Sancti Leodegarii, and in 1339, Assheby Leger. The addition refers to the church dedication of St Leger, in Latin *Leodegarius*.

Minor names here include Foxholes, which refers to where the hunt would often make a temporary camp, while Grove Farm was marked out by its 'grove of trees'.

The local here is the Old Coach House Inn, a name which is self-explanatory, although the addition of 'Old' in a pub name is always greeted with scepticism for most often it refers to 'older', not exactly misleading but used in the hope of attracting business, as 'old' pubs are seemingly more desirable.

The manor house at Ashby St Ledgers was the home of the Catesby family for several generations. During the early seventeenth century, it was an important meeting place for the conspirators in the Gunpowder Plot.

ASHLEY

As with the previous name, this is also a common name, found throughout the land. Always derived from Old English *aesc* and *leah*, it refers to '(the place) in the clearing of the ash trees'. If the places so named were closer, they would doubtless have acquired a second distinctive element.

ASHTON

There are two places in the county of this name, each with similar but not identical meanings. The major surprise is that they lack a distinguishing second element found with many other Ashtons.

That found near Oundle is listed in 1086 as *Ascetone*, and is derived from Old English *aesc* and *tun* or 'the farmstead of or by the ash trees'.

The second is not far from Towcester and comes from the plural form of Old English *aesc*, telling us of '(the place at) the ash trees' and recorded as Asce in 1086 and Asshen in 1296. Here too is Gun Hole, a place found near a bridge and almost certainly a corruption of the person who was here to charge for passage across the bridge and thus maintain it. Perhaps it comes as a surprise to find this was the responsibility of one Gunhild, a Saxon woman.

ASTCOTE

While Domesday's record of Aviescote may seem closer to the modern form than the later listings as Hauekescote and Hauescote in 1198 and 1316 respectively, all point to the same origin. This is an Old English name derived from a Saxon personal name with the suffix *cot*, giving 'Aefic's cottages'.

ASTROP

Listed in 1200 as Estorp and in 1270 as Estrop, the Old English and Old Scandinavian *trop* and *torp*, discussed under Althorp, is seen once more. This is clearly 'the eastern outlying farmstead', from Old English *east* and *throp*. Furthermore, we are also told where the name originated: the settlement west of here, which may well have been the original home. It is likely that Astrop began life as an outlying farming settlement used only in the growing season, which grew to become a permanent and independent community.

This name is a clear indication of how neighbouring settlements gave a name to a place. For the earliest occupants, there was no lavish naming ceremony; to them, it was simply home. This explains why there are so many personal names, descriptions of the area and, as in this example, directional references found in place names.

ASTWELL

A name recorded as Estwelle in Domesday, a name referring to this being the '(place at) the eastern stream'.

Falcutt appears from the thirteenth century, a name from *feawe cot*, which may literally be 'few cottages' but is thought to be stating these were 'humble cottages'. Stockings Farm has a common name, one which comes from Old English *stocking* or 'the place marked by tree stumps'.

AVON, RIVER

This river is most often described as the Warwickshire Avon, there being at least four significant rivers of this name in England alone. This name comes from a British word meaning simply 'river', a word which is unknown directly, for there is no written form. However, we can understand this as it is related to Welsh *afon*, Cornish *avon*, and Irish *abhann*, all with identical meanings. Even today, it is not unusual for us to refer to the local river as simply 'the river', thus, in days when the locals hardly travelled any distance at all, such names were inevitable.

AYNHO

An unusual-sounding name only because it features the Old English suffix *hoh*, normally only found in minor names. Recorded as Aienho 1086, Eynho 1220, and Ainho 1226, this is '(the place at) Aega's spur of land'.

Pesthouse Wood was named after the nearby 'hospital for contagious diseases', which could once be found here; Smanhill Covert grew on 'the smooth hill' which gave it its name; College Farm is on land once a possession of Magdalen College, Oxford; and Puckwell must have been the place of legends, for this is 'the goblin's spring'.

One local benefactor has done more to name streets of Aynho than any other. William Ralph Cartwright built cottages for farm labourers, and in the 1820s, the Red Lion changed its name to the Cartwright Arms. The family can trace their ancestry here back to the sixteenth century; however, while we know plenty about the man, unfortunately, no record was kept of the inspiration behind him naming Paradise Row, Spring Gardens, Hart Lane and Wapping, although the family were the reason for the naming of the road known as Cartwright Gardens.

The local pub here is the Great Western Arms, recalling the two stations in the town, which were both served by the GWR, and while both had closed to trains by 1964, the buildings still stand and are now private houses.

Chapter 2

Badby–Byfield

BADBY

As discussed under Althorp, the county had influences from both the Saxon and Scandinavian cultures and its place names reflect this. Listings of Badby are found as aet Baddan byrig 792, Baddan by 944, Badebi 1086, and Baddanbyr 1356. As can be seen, the eighth-century record has a different suffix, which comes from Old English *burh* and not Old Scandinavian *by* meaning 'village'. This is 'Badda's fortified place', featuring a Saxon personal name.

Public houses here include the Windmill, reflecting a former sight in the village. The Maltsters Country Inn not only refers to brewing, but also suggests a rural location, both of which are clearly advertising the product and the location.

BARBY

Unlike the previous name, this is one of Scandinavian beginnings and therefore the place must have been founded by Norsemen. Records date back to Domesday as Berchebi, later found as Bergebi and Bereweby in the early thirteenth century. This is from *berg by* and speaks of 'the village on or of the hills'.

Local names include Chapel Farm, named after the old chapel found at Olney Manor; the name of the manor is itself from the place name and the settlement known as 'Ona's woodland clearing'.

BARNACK

Today a part of Lincolnshire but historically in Northamptonshire. Listed as Beornican in 972, as Bernak in 1050, Bernac in 1086, Berneca in 1163, Bernech in 1167, and Bernek in 1202, this comes from Old English to describe 'Beorn's *wics* or specialised farms' and probably dairy farms.

The local name of Hills and Holes describes the naturally broken ground, while Pilsgate refers to 'Pil's gate or gap'.

BARTON SEAGRAVE

This is a common place name which almost without exception points to the Old English *bere tun* or 'the barley farm'. Only two records of this name of note, as Bertone in 1086

Bartholomew Arms at Blakesley.

and as Barton Segrave in 1412. This fifteenth-century record is the first to show any addition: a surprisingly late development. It refers to a Nicholas de Segrave, who held part of this estate by 1314.

While the hunt is currently banned in England, the traditional meeting place of the pub still shows in such names as the Stirrup Cup. This was the drink offered to the Master of the Hounds as the hunt were ready to depart, usually port or sherry, and was also applied to the distinctive vessel in which it was served.

BENEFIELD

A name found as Beringafeld in 970, Benefeld in 1086, Benifeld in 1130, and as Berifeld in 1236. Here is a Saxon personal name and Old English *feld*, which describes 'Bera's open land'.

Biggin Hall was built on the site of an earlier construction, as evidenced by the name meaning 'the building'. Swallow Holes points to a place where nine natural holes allow the land to flood and drain with the seasons. Banhaw Wood tells us it was 'the spur of land where beans grow'.

BLAKESLEY

A place first recorded in 1086 as Blaculveslea, with later forms in 1190 as Blaculfeslea and 1203 as Blacolvesle. Here, the Saxon personal name is followed by the common

Old English suffix *leah*, telling us it was '(the place) at the woodland glade associated with Blaecwulf'.

The name of Seawell Farm is derived from the 'seven springs' which are found here. The local pub is the Bartholomew Arms, while opposite we find Bartholomew Gardens, both remember the family who owned the local hall from 1876 to 1919. In 1903, C. W. Bartholomew built a 15-inch narrow gauge railway, which linked the hall to the nearby station, three quarters of a mile away. Hauling coal, farm supplies, the occasional passenger, and patients when the hall was a hospital during the First World War, it lasted until 1940, when the track was lifted to rework its metal, while the hall itself was demolished in 1957.

BLATHERWYCKE

The most unusual aspect of this name is how it has not been corrupted into something much shorter and/or easier to pronounce. It appears in 1086 as Blarewiche, in 1203 as Blatherwic, and in 1227 as Bladrewyc, all of which show a personal name followed by the Old English *wic*. This seems to suggest 'the farm where bladder-plants grow'; however, the two elements are difficult to see together. The suffix is a term used to refer to a specialised farm, in virtually all instances a dairy farm. If the definition is correct, then perhaps the idea of bladder-plants being farmed is erroneous and the two elements, although they apply to the region, are otherwise unrelated.

Britain Sale does not mean what it seems today, for this refers to this area being held by Ralph Brito in 1227, while *sale* is a dialect term referring to a division of a wood where the underwood was frequently cut and sold. Cadge Wood features the term *cadge*, which refers to a 'frame where several hawks are carried and sold'. While Hostage Wood is a corruption of *haespe hecg* and refers to a 'lockable enclosure'.

BLISWORTH

The place is listed in Domesday as Blidesworde and a century later is found as Blitheswurde. Both records show the name to be Saxon or Old English in origin, featuring *worth* preceded by a personal name, and meaning 'Blith's enclosure'.

One local name is that of the Loundes, a name from Old Norse *lundr* or 'woodland grove'.

Here is the Royal Oak, one of the most popular pub names in the country. It is named after the Boscobel Oak, at Shifnal in Shropshire, where Charles II and his aide Colonel Carless hid while escaping Parliamentarian forces after the Battle of Worcester. His return to the country and the Restoration of the monarchy was marked by the creation of Royal Oak Day, 29 May, the King's birthday. Many pubs take the name of trees, most often referring to one which stood outside. This was seen in the case of the Walnut Tree Inn.

Nearby, the Grand Union Canal heads towards Stoke Bruerne and, to avoid a long detour around the hills, cuts right through via a tunnel. At first, workers made an error and there was a dog leg in the route; however, three years later, this route collapsed, killing fourteen men. Thus a different tunnel was cut and, when it opened on 25 March 1805, was the third longest canal tunnel in the country and is still the ninth longest in the world at 3,076 yards, reaching 143 feet underground at its deepest point.

Bozeat's attractive village sign.

BODDINGTON (UPPER & LOWER)

Domesday records this place name as Botendon, a name from a Saxon personal name and Old English *dun* and describing 'the hill of a man called Boda'. The additions are self-explanatory.

Spella House was constructed on the place that gave it a name, that of 'speech hill', which describes where meetings were held. Significant rocks and stones were often used to mark boundaries and few can have been more important than that which marked the point where Northamptonshire, Warwickshire and Oxfordshire meet and which is known as Three Shires Stone.

The rural location is reflected in the name of the Plough Inn, an easily recognisable image. The Carpenters Arms is one of the most common trade names for a pub, trades being popular for early landlords, who often provided two services.

BOZEAT

Domesday's record of Bosiete is not as helpful in defining this name as the twelfth-century records of Bosegete and Bosezate. The suffix to the personal name here is the Old English *geat*, an element that is normally seen today as 'gate'. The meaning of gate was not the same historically as it is today. In the modern era, the gate is either an access

Brackley welcome sign.

point or a means of denying entry or exit. Historically, it was the road that ran to and from the destination, effectively still the means of access but referring to the route. This makes the definition of 'Bosa's gate' easier to envisage.

The Red Lion is the most common pub name in the land, symbolising Scotland and also, prior to that, John of Gaunt, the most powerful man in England during the fourteenth century.

BRACKLEY

No less than four records of this place name, Brachelai (1086), Brackelea (1173), Bracchela (1182), and Brackeley (1230), yet none make the personal name very certain. Here, the suffix is the Old English *leah*, a common enough element and telling us of the '(place at) the woodland clearing of a man called Bracca'.

Here is St Rumbald's Well, named after the saint who was born in AD 662. He is said to have spoken at birth, requested baptism, declared his strong faith and, on the third day of his life, given a stirring sermon, after which he died.

Local pubs include the Reindeer Inn, an easily recognised image and rarely symbolising anyone or anything. The Manor represents the former manor house; the Stratton Arms marks the family of Alderman John Locke Stratton, who served as mayor between 1890 and 1897. With nearby Silverstone and its famous racing circuit, one pub here took the name of the Chequered Flag, while another shows it is only 200 yards from the railway station by its name of the Locomotive Inn.

BRADDEN

From Domesday's Bradene in 1086, through to the thirteenth-century records of Braddene, Bradenden, and Bradden, the origin is clearly Old English *brade denu*. These two elements are common to many place names but are not often found in combination, although there must certainly be many settlements founded in the 'broad valley'.

Bury Brake is probably a reminder of this manor being held by Agnes de Bery.

BRAFIELD-ON-THE-GREEN

The several records of this name found in the eleventh, twelfth and thirteenth centuries all point to an Old English origin of *bragen feld*. The suffix *feld* is the root word for the modern 'field' and, although they are both open agricultral land, they are not the same thing. A field is enclosed, typically by a hedgerow or perhaps a wall or fence, and has a gate which prevents livestock escaping or entering to dine on the crops. The *feld* was also used to grow crops and even for grazing animals but was simply cleared land. This name tells us it was '(the place at) the open country near higher ground' and was happy to be just that until the sixteenth century, when the addition first appeared and stuck.

BRAMPTON ASH

Listed as Brantone in Domesday and as Bramton in 1220, this name comes from Old English *brom tun* and describes 'the farmstead where broom grew'. The addition, necessary for such a common place name, refers to 'ash trees'.

BRAUNSTON

Listed in 956 as Brantestun and in 1086 as Branteston, this is a name which is derived from an Old English personal name followed by the most common element in English place names, *tun*, which is seen as a 'farming community' or, more accurately, refers to the buidlings themselves and therefore 'farmstead'. This is a name also found in neighbouring counties and is always 'Brant's farmstead'.

Here we also find Braunstone Cleves, the addition from *fealh clif*, which is understood as 'the ploughed hill'. Berryfields comes from *burh feld* or 'the fortification at the open land'; Langdon House was built on 'the long hill slope'; and Northfield House was at 'the northern hill slope'.

19

Pubs here include the Admiral Nelson, named to commemorate England's greatest hero and the one individual who has had more pubs named after him than any other. Early landlords needed to have more than one string to their bow: hence the Wheatsheaf Arms depicts this image on the coat of arms of the Worshipful Company of Bakers. The Old Plough Inn is a common name, for it suggests a rural location and, even as a silhouette, is easily recognised in times when the population was largely illiterate.

Here is the junction of the Grand Union and Oxford Canals, once a major point on the canal system.

BRAYBROOKE

A place name taken, somewhat obviously, from the water course, which flowed through the community and provided a source of fresh water. The name of the place is recorded as Bradebroc in 1086, as Braibroc in 1163, and as Brabroc in 1197 and is from the Old English *brad broc* or 'the broad brook'. However, this is the meaning of the stream name, and the settlement should correctly be defined as the '(place at) the broad brook'.

Eckland Lodge has its origins in Old Scandinavian *eil lundr* and describes 'the oak wood'. Two former residents of Braybrooke Castle are remembered in the names of Griffin Road and Latymer Close.

BRIGSTOCK

Plenty of eleventh- and twelfth-century listings of this name, all of which show this to be from the Old English *brycg stoc* meaning 'the place of or by the bridge'.

Some attention should be given to the Old English *stoc*, which, for many years, was defined as 'special place'. Aside from the elements that feature as a suffix, it must be the most common element in place names in England; it is certainly the most common place name in England, which is why so many feature an addition. That such is no longer offered as being a 'special place' was quite predictable; anything is special to certain individuals, and for a place to be accepted as 'special', we really need some idea just what was special about it. Obviously, the first thought is religious, yet the local meeting place, trading point or wedding venue would have been equally as special. Without knowledge of what made it stand out, it was deemed wrong to describe it as such.

Local names of note include Cherry Lap, recorded as Shenelelappe in 1300 and referring to 'the bright clearing in the detached district'. Harely Way may refer to either 'the boundary woodland clearing' or perhaps this is 'the woodland clearing where hares are seen'. Stubby Stiles refers to a path and/or stile near a place that had been stubbed or had had most of the growth removed and has just the bare minimum of the shrubs or trees remaining.

Mounterley Wood gives a good description of the trees found here, which must have been well matured, for this describes a place where wooden beams were cut for lintels, hence the name literally means 'mantel trees'. Stephen Oak Riding is so named for it traditionally being a place where King Stephen (1096-1154) was positioned when he shot down a deer while out hunting.

Pubs here include the Green Dragon, the heraldic image for the earls of Pembroke.

BRIXWORTH

Listings of this name are many: Domesday's *Briclesworde*, in 1160 as Bricleswurde, in 1198 as Brihteswurthe, and in 1224 as Brikelesworth. The suffix is Saxon *worth*, meaning 'enclosure', which is preceded by a personal name. Although these individuals are unknown, as is their relevance to the place, based on the knowledge of how the English language evolved, we are able to have some idea of what these names were. Here we find 'the enclosure of a man called Beorhtel or Bricel'. While these names may seem very different, think of how difficult it would be in the future to discern between Michael, Mike, Mikey, Mick, Micky, Mitchell, or even Michaela and Michelle.

The local name of Wolfage describes 'the wolf hedge', that is one constructed to keep them out and, presumably, away from their livestock.

The Coach & Horses suggests this was a stopping place for the transportation routes, while the George Inn can refer to any of the first four kings of England called George who reigned from 1714 to 1830, although a play on words for Georgian cannot be discounted.

BROCKHALL

In 1086, the name was given as *Brocole* and, by 1220, was Brochole. These are from the Old English *brocc hol*, which may not be too difficult to see as '(place at) a badger hole' – literally, a sett. The term 'badger' is a comparatively recent one, the traditional name of 'Brock' for a badger is derived from that original word much the same as Tod is the ancient word for the fox.

BROUGHTON

A rather more common place name than one would suppose, with over thirty major places of this name plus many others as minor names. One reason there are so many examples is there are three distinctly different origins; indeed, many of these origins are blurred and it is difficult to see which is the true beginning.

This Northamptonshire Broughton is listed in 1086 as Burtone and in 1125 as Brohtune, a name which originates from Old English or Saxon *burh tun* giving us 'the farmstead with or near the fortification'.

The local name of Clarke's Lodge remembers former tenant Edward Clark and his family, who were here by 1702. The Sun Inn today sends a message of warmth and welcome; historically, it was simply a very simple sign.

In July 1826, the Midsummer Fair here was the scene of a pitched battle. For some years, George Catherall, who liked to be known as Captain Slash, gave up the chance of a comfortable and well-established family life for one of crime. His mother, appalled by his decision, told him his choice would be the death of him and that he would die with his shoes on (i.e., not peacefully in bed).

Catherall assembled a collection of rogues and ruffians; numbering around one hundred, they targeted county fairs and other such large gatherings. However, this Midsummer Fair proved their undoing, for the stallholders and locals were prepared and armed and fought back. This resulted in the arrest of Captain Slash and six of his cohorts. One was transported for life, five received substantial sentences, and the ringleader was given a death sentence.

The sentence was carried out on 21 July. With the noose around his neck and shortly before the executioner let him drop, Captain Slash kicked off his shoes into the watching crowd. Seconds later, he died having proved his mother's prophecy wrong.

On the second Sunday in December each year, in those first few moments of the new day, the chimes of midnight are drowned by the sound of the Broughton Tin Can Band. This age-old custom involves various members of the community taking up their instruments and playing for an hour.

Whether this qualifies as 'music' is debatable, for it sounds just like a group of individuals marching around the town banging dustbin lids, buckets, pots, pans, buckets, rattling stones in biscuit tins, accompanied by whistles, whoops and shrieks – indeed, this is exactly what it is. The tour takes in all parts of the village; hence the performance can be 'enjoyed' by all residents.

The origins are unclear, most often said to be to banish evil spirits or vagrants from the village. However, there is a clear resemblance to the tradition of 'rough music', a loud and unmelodic racket forced upon any house where known wife-beaters or philanderers were known to reside: a warning to the man to either desist or leave. Oddly, the same actions were aimed at men who were hen-pecked or, worse, cuckolded.

BUGBROOKE

Records of this name include Buchebroc in 1086, Bukebroc in 1201, and Buckebrok in 1247. The most likely origin for this name is '(place at) the brook of a man called Bucca'. However, there is a small chance the first element might refer to deer or 'bucks'.

Corporation Farm was a possession of the Corporation of Northampton, while Littlelift Farm stands where there was a small *hlip* or 'leap', a wicker gate or gap designed to permit the passage of wild animals such as deer but stopping domestic livestock.

The Bakers Arms remind us that landlords often performed another service to the community, here featuring the coat of arms granted in the sixteenth century.

BURTON LATIMER

In 1086, it is recorded as Burtone, and by 1228, it is Burton, although the first mention of the addition is as late as 1482 with Burton Latymer. The basic name comes from Old English *burh tun* telling us of 'the farmstead with or near a fortification'. The addition refers to the manor being held by the Latimer family, who were here from the thirteenth century, although their name was not used for the place for another two centuries.

Buccleuch Farm was associated with the Duke of Buccleuch by 1803.

The Waggon and Horses was the main method of moving large loads between sites, while the innkeeper often acted as an agent. Note the spelling of 'Waggon' is the accepted British spelling, although the alternative, 'Wagon', is seen more and more often. The Olde Victoria stands near Victoria Street, predictably named after the queen. It is

Welcome to Burton Latimer.

interesting to note that the additional 'Olde' tells us it cannot be that old, for such was never used before the latter half of the eighteenth century. The Duke Arms is named after Duke Street, thought to represent the Duke of Wellington.

Street names include Addis Close, after Jack Addis, a long-serving figure in the local Scout movement. Ashby Close remembers Douglas Ashby, who combined working for the church and the parish council with a lifetime preparing the history of his beloved Burton Latimer. Barlow Court is named after the family, who included Charles, Frank, Alfred and Roland Barlow, three generations of councillors whose family served the community via a cake shop, and as butchers, drapers, grocers, builders, miners of ironstone, brickmakers, and farmers. The Burton Ironstone Company was managed by Thomas Bird, who is remembered by Bird Street.

Coles Close is situated on the site of the former Coles Boot Company, which had closed around 1978. Croxen Close is where the brickworks of the nineteenth-century company owned by John Croxen were situated. Denton Court remembers the farming Denton family. Eady Road commemorates the family of farmers, shepherds, millers, shopkeepers and market gardeners whose link with Burton Latimer can be traced back as early as 1539. Hollands Drive is on land once farmed by Vincent Holland. Bridle Road was, long before it was surfaced and houses built, a long-established bridle path.

Jacques Road remembers the Reverend William Baldwin Jacques, vicar of St Mary's from 1895 to 1911. His wife owned some land here and, when her son was tragically killed in action in 1916, she paid for two bells, one to commemorate her son and the second her husband. Whitney Road and Westley Close remember Henry Whitney and Joseph Westley respectively, co-founders of Whitney & Westley, a shoemaking concern which provided many with employment.

Churchill Way was cut in 1965, the year former prime minister Sir Winston Churchill died. George Street was first seen in 1937, the year of the coronation of George VI. Queensway was developed in the early part of the reign of Queen Elizabeth II. Duke Street is named after the Duke's Arms Inn, Newman Street after the Newman family, of whom Alfred was landlord in the late nineteenth century. The Newmans were landowners and staunch Liberal supporters, and thus, when the land was given over to development, suggested Rosebery Street be named in honour of the prime minister, Earl of Rosebery.

Lanson Close was named after Clive Lawson, who gave thirty-six years service to the Urban District Council. Mackintosh Close remembers Bob Mackintosh, a councillor with over thirty years service. Meads Court remembers the Meads family, who had a dairy business in the town for over eighty years. Laurie Sturgess was clerk to the town council, and had Sturgess Court named after him.

Councillor Arthur Gambrell Miller, also landlord of the Thatcher Arms, gave his name to Miller Road. Morby Court is for Councillor Albert Morby, who served in that capacity for over thirty years. Woodcock Street remembers William G. Woodcock, company secretary of the Burton Ironstone Company. York Close is for Councillor Marion York, who died in 2004 after many years of loyal service. Theme names include the princess theme seen with Alice Drive, Diana Way, and Grace Court.

Brooks Close is named after Nurse Agnes Brooks, midwife in the town for forty-three years. She cycled around the town from 1925, later upgrading to the first of several black Hillman cars, which became her trademark as much as the black Labrador dogs which she could be seen walking when not at work. Retiring in 1968, she lived in Williams Road every day of her life in Burton Latimer until her death in 1971.

Home to a number of industries over the years, Tweed Close is a reminder that worsted cloth was made here, while the Weetabix factory proved inspirational for the names of Wheatfield Drive, Barley Drive, Oathill Rise, and Cornfield Way.

BYFIELD

The earliest listing of this name dates from the time of Domesday as Bifelde; later records mirror this form. This would seem to be Old English *bi feld* or the place 'by the open land', which suggests there was once another element describing what place was here.

Locally, we find the name of Ludwell, which takes its name from 'the loud spring'; Westhorp was 'the westerly outlying farmstead'; and Dodd's Barn was home to the family of William Dodd from at least 1629.

The Cross Tree public house took the name of the prominent tree which stood here, itself a road marker.

Chapter 3

Caldecott–Culworth

CALDECOTT

A name found in several counties around the eastern-central area of England, all from Old English *cald cot*, giving 'the cold or inhospitable cottages'. What is most surprising is how little any of these names have changed over the centuries.

CANONS ASHBY

As stated under Ashby St Ledgers, the name of Ashby is one of the most common in the land and additions should be expected. Normally, such additions follow the name; however, sometimes they precede it.

The name is recorded as Ascebi in 1086 and, for the first time with the addition, in 1254 as Esseby Canonicorum. The basic name, as with all Ashbys, is from the Old English/Old Scandinavian combination of *aesc* and *by* meaning 'the village of or by the ash trees'. The addition refers to the founding of the priory here in the twelfth century.

Locally, we find Conduit Covert, a name which tells us this was where pipes fed spring water directly into the convent, while Wards Copse was home to the family of John le Warde by 1316.

CAR DIKE

Found as Karisdik in 1245 and as Carisdick in 1340, this is a continuation of that in South Lincolnshire. This either comes from the Old Scandinavian personal name *Karr*, which was associated with the ancient earthwork, or perhaps this is an early Middle English *kerre* or 'marshland'.

CASTLE ASHBY

Another Ashby, and another origin of 'the village of or by the ash trees'. The addition here is first seen in 1361 as Castel Assheby and there was once a castle here.

Locally, we find the name of Chadstone, itself derived from 'Ceadd's farmstead'.

Left: Porters Lodge at Castle Ashby.

Below: Station Road, Castle Ashby.

CASTOR

Historically considered a part of Northamptonshire, this name is recorded as Cyneburge caestre in 948, Castra in 972, and Castre in 1086. The modern name is from Old English *caestre* and describes 'the Roman stronghold'.

Belsize Farm was settled at 'the beautiful spot', while Normangate Field is at 'the Norseman's gate or gap'. In Castor Field are two stones known as Robin Hood and Little John which, while they do show arrow nicks in their tops, most likely represent a marker for the road from Bernack to the Gunwade Ferry in order for them to avoid the toll road. The arrow nicks are explained as being a mark of respect to St Edmund, this area being named after the saint who was killed by Danish arrows.

CATESBY

Recorded in Domesday as Catesbi, this is from an Old Scandinavian personal name and *by* to describe 'the village of a man called Katr or Kati'.

Locally, we find Catwell Barn, which has often been said to be from 'wild cat hill'; however, this does not stand up to examination. The Scottish wild cat never lived here: the habitat does not suit this creature. Furthermore, they are highly territorial and solitary animals, as indeed are all of the cat family, with the exception of lions and they only tolerate each other's presence as they live together as sisters, nieces and aunts, while the numbers are necessary in order to bring down their large prey. On the subject of prey, no matter how many cats lived here, there would need to be even more rodents, their principal prey. Assuming a cat eats one rodent most days in a single year, there would be 300 times as many rodents as felines – this would be 'the stream land infested by mice'. Hence, this is most likely a personal name, 'Cat's stream', and probably a nickname.

Newbold Grounds Farm was the site of 'the new building'; Ryton Hill is from *ryge dun* and 'the hill where rye grows'; Steppington Hill is from *steap hyll* and 'at the steep hill'; and Dane Hole is probably derived from folklore etymology, for there is no record of any Danes here.

CAT'S WATER

This is an important boundary, a dyke, between the counties of Northamptonshire and Cambridgeshire. It is recorded as Cattewater in the fourteenth century and le Cateswater in 1504, which can only be the name of the owner, for the animal is never found in sufficient numbers to have a place named after it.

CHACOMBE

Listings of this name include Cewecumbe (1086), Cahucumba (1166), and Chacombe (1195). Here is a Saxon or Old English name telling us of '(the place at) Ceawa's valley', the personal name being suffixed by *cumb*.

CHAPEL BRAMPTON

Brampton is a name which comes from Old English *brom tun* or 'the farmstead where broom grows'. This is a fairly common name and requires the addition for distinction. Clearly, the name refers to the place of worship, deemed a 'chapel' to differ from Church Brampton and seen from the thirteenth century.

The name of Hoe Hill is derived from *hoh*, a Saxon word describing 'the spur of land'. Here we find Merry Tom Lane, named after the favourite horse of John, the 5th Earl Spencer (1835-1910), always known as the Red Earl on account of his long red beard. Out fox hunting one day, he attempted to leap the River Nene and the poor horse broke its neck. The name of the lane is probably taken from the monument the earl had erected to mark the burial place of Merry Tom.

CHARWELTON

Found as Cerweltone and Cerweltona in 1086 and 1110, there can be no doubt this is 'the farmstead on the river Cherwell'. See under the river name for an examination of the origins. Cherwell Farm also takes the name of the local river.

Fox Hall Farm may well have been built where foxes were known to be found and would have been taken during the hunt, while Sharman's Hill is named after the local family of Sherman, who are recorded living nearby.

CHELVESTON

Domesday lists the name as Celuestone in 1086; however, just 120 years later, the only other early form is exactly as today. This Saxon personal name precedes Old English *tun*, telling us this was 'Ceolwulf's farmstead'.

The local is the Star & Garter, a public house name which refers to the Most Noble Order of the Garter, created by Edward III in the fourteenth century, which is always limited to twenty-five members, including the reigning monarch. It is said to have originated at a court ball when the King noticed a garter fall from the apparently elegant leg of the Countess of Salisbury. Picking up the garter, he noted he was being eyed by many in the room, upon which he placed the item on his own leg stating '*Honi soit qui mal y pense*' – this is now the motto of the order, meaning 'Evil be to him who evil thinks'.

CHERWELL, RIVER

A name recorded as Ceruelle in 1200 and as Charwelle in 1247, this name has proven difficult to understand. The second element here is undoubtedly Old English *wella* meaning 'spring or stream' and likely refers to the river near its source when it is still very young. However, the first element has never been understood, for it does not seem to be a personal name, nor can it be identified with a descriptive term for the river. This is possibly a second river name, that of a tributary and therefore associated with

Welsh *car* and used to describe 'the pleasant river', or perhaps this is related to Old Scandinavian *kar*, which would describe the 'hollow gorge' through which the tributary descended to join the main river.

CHIPPING WARDEN

Two parts to this name, the basic name here being the second half. Records date from 1066 when the place was listed as Werdun, in 1086, it is seen as Waredone, and in 1387, Chepyng Wardoun. This name is derived from the Old English *weard-dun*, the 'watch or look-out hill'. The addition is another Old English term, *ceping*, speaking of the 'market'. Oddly, the name referring to the market is not seen today until almost the end of the fourteenth century, and yet the grant which allowed the market was rescinded and abolished in 1227. The obvious explanation is that earlier records of the name with the addition have not survived to the twenty-first century. However, it would be interesting to discover just when the addition first appeared, either when it was granted or because it was cancelled.

Wallow Bank had already referred to itself as 'the bank at the projection of land', from *wall hoh*, before the addition of the second part. Both Trafford House and Trafford Bridge share the name of 'the trap ford', where a trap for fish was set up to provide a supply of protein for the table.

CHURCH BRAMPTON

As with Chapel Brampton, this is 'the farmstead where broom grows', with the addition of the religious reference from the thirteenth century.

CLAY COTON

The earliest eleventh-century listings give the name as simply Cotes, which has evolved in the plural 'cottages'. By 1284, it has become Cleycotes and, in 1329, Claycotone; the addition is from the Old English *claeg*, telling us of 'the cottages in the clayey area'.

CLIFFE FOREST

A part of the larger Rockingham Forest and the area which takes its name from King's Cliffe. This name comes from Old English *clif* and describes the '(place at) the cliff or bank'.

CLIPSTON

Records of Clipestone in 1086, Clipestona in 1155, and in the modern form as early as 1202. Here is an example of a hybrid name, a combination of an Old Scandinavian personal name and an Old English suffix in *tun*. Such are not unusual in the region of England influenced by both cultures; however, these places almost exclusively feature a personal name. It is easier for a name in the form of an individual to be transferred from one culture to another than it is for a basic word. Here, the place name tells us of 'the farmstead of a man called Klyppr or Klippr'.

Longhold Lodge takes its name from 'the long weald', and Twantry Farm must have been marked by 'two trees'.

COGENHOE

In Domesday, the place is recorded as Cugenho and, in 1236, as Cugeho. Here, the origin is a Saxon personal name with Old English *hoh*, giving us 'the hill-spur of a man named Cugga'.

The local pub is the Royal Oak, named after the tree in which King Charles II hid after the Battle of Worcester, thus escaping capture by the enemy soldiers. What had once been acres of orchard and open fields has recently been developed, the street names referring to the history of the place: Orchard Way, for the orchards, Glebe Road, a small farming area, and St Peters Way, from the dedication of the church.

COLD ASHBY

Another 'Ashby', again derived from *aesc-by* or 'the village of or by the ash trees'. Here, this common place name is given distinction by the addition of Old English *cald*, literally 'cold' but more likely to suggest 'exposed'. The name is recorded in 1086 as Essebi and by 1150 as Caldessebi.

Here is Chilcote's Cover, the only reminder of the old Domesday manor of Cildecote, which was still a viable settlement as late as 1235 as Childecote. This name comes from *cild cote* and describes 'the cottages of the young men or servants'. The name of Portly Ford Bridge is a corruption of the Portway, the road which crosses here and which is from *port weg* or 'the market or traders' road'.

Cold Ashby is claimed to be the highest village in the county.

COLD HIGHAM

Hardly seems necessary to offer the meaning of the first element here, except to say it is derived from the Old English or Saxon *cald*, although more likely telling us it was 'exposed'. The only old records of note are Hecham, recorded as such in 1086, 1198 and 1254, so this would seem to be very close to the original. Indeed it is from *heah-ham*, meaning 'the high homestead'.

The name of Potcote tells us it was the site of 'the cottages in a depression', while Grimscote could be one of two possible origins depending upon whether this was Old English 'Grim's cottages' or Old Scandinavian 'Grimr's cottages'.

COLLINGTREE

Records of this name have been found as Colestrev and Colentrev in 1086, Colintrie in 1163, and Coluntre in 1251. This is an Old English personal name followed by *treow* and means 'Cola's tree'.

Similar forms of other place names are found elsewhere, always giving a name such as Cola, Colan, or Kolan before a tree. No deity of such a name is known, yet it must certainly have been a woodland spirit or similar figure.

COLLYWESTON

In 1086, this place is recorded as Weston and, in 1309, as Colynweston. The basic name is derived from the Old English or Saxon *west-tun*, meaning 'the western farmstead'. Such a basic name is, somewhat predictably, a common place name and thus merits the addition for distinction. Unlike so many others, this addition has joined with the basic name and formed a single noun. A second oddity of this manorial name sees it come from the Christian name and not the family; the gentleman in question is Nicholas de Segrave, who was here in the thirteenth century. The third oddity of this name is that the pet form Colin has been used, not Nicholas itself. Few place names can have been named after a specific individual and can have told us how he was known by his friends and family.

The local pub reflects the importance of slate to the area. Also seen in the name of Slater Lane, the pub goes by the name of the Collyweston Slater. Here are two long-distance footpaths: Hereward Way is 110 miles, named after Hereward the Wake, traditionally the last remnant of organised resistance against William the Conqueror; and Jurassic Way, 88 miles along the limestone ridge laid down in the geological period which gave it a name.

CORBY

Records of this name date from 1066 when it is listed as Corebi, followed by Corbei in 1086, Corbi in 1167, and Coreby in 1168. This is a name of Old Scandinavian derivation, the personal name preceding *by*, the Norse equivalent of the Saxon *tun*. This place began life as 'Kori's village'.

Occupation Farm tells us that this was once tenanted.

Local pubs take their names from many sources. The Cardigan Arms remind us of the earls of Cardigan who lived on the estate at nearby Deene Park, the 7th Earl of Cardigan having led the Charge of the Light Brigade at Balaklava, while the Rockingham Arms similarly refers to Rockingham Castle, although the Everard Arms refers to the name of the brewery.

The Open Hearth is a reminder of Corby's steel industry, it being used in the smelting process, while also suggesting a nice, warm domestic fire. Similarly, the Corby Candle is a reminder of the fire which produced the heat to extract the ore. The image of the Shirehouse is diplayed outside the pub of that name; the Hazel Tree is named from that landmark which stood outside; the Phoenix is always an indication that this pub has

Elizabeth Street, Corby – one of a number of 'royal' street names.

Charles Street, Corby.

been refurbished or reopened, much as the fabled bird is reborn every 500 years from its own ashes; the Talisman is a lucky charm; the Square Peg refers to the peg which taps the wooden barrel; and the Spread Eagle is a common symbol favoured by both the Roman legions and seen as forming the pulpit in many churches.

Roads to the east of Corby include that which reminds us of the town's industry in Steel Road. Nearby, we find Hubble Road, named after astronomer Edwin Hubble (1889-1953);

Crick Close, from Francis Crick (1916-2004), the co-discoverer of the structure of the DNA molecule, who was born in the county at Weston Flavell; Royce Close, is a reminder of Sir Frederick Henry Royce (1863-1933), half of the Rolls-Royce partnership who produced the epitome of style in a motor car; Lister Close remembers Joseph Lister (1827-1912), whose work revolutionised surgery by the introduction of sterilisation techniques he developed; Stephenson Way is clearly after George Stephenson (1781-1848), the renowned Father of the Railways; James Watt Avenue is after James Watt (1736-1819), who greatly improved the Newcomen steam engine; Whitworth Avenue remembers Joseph Whitworth (1803-87), who developed the first true standardised screw thread; and Telfords Lane is after Thomas Telford (1757-1834), a Scottish civil engineer who is best remembered for canals, but who also designed the Menai Suspension Bridge and the A5; he also gave his name to the town in Shropshire.

Another theme is of Scottish place names, a diverse collection which includes Scapa Road, after Scapa Flow, a body of water off the Orkney Islands and the nation's chief naval base during both world wars; Harris Road is after the Hebridean island of Lewis and Harris, the largest island in the group other than the main islands of Britain and Ireland; Mull Drive refers to the Mull of Kintyre, a headland of Scotland which was immortalised in the song which became the first to sell over 2 million copies in the UK; Shetland Way, after the Shetland Islands, the group of around 300 islands off northern Scotland of which only thirteen are inhabited; Skye Road, after the island of the Inner Hebrides, which is now connected to the mainland by a bridge; and Fyfe Road is named after the former county of Scotland, although this should correctly be spelled Fife!

Ships of the Royal Navy provided the names of Hood Court, Collingwood Avenue, Duncan Road, Beatty Gardens, Duckworth Road, Howard Avenue, Raleigh Close, Rodney Drive, and Howe Crescent.

The royal family is seen in the names of a number of roads near the town centre. Queen Victoria's daughter Princess Louise became Marchioness of Lorne and Duchess of Argyll, when she married the Governor-General of Canada, who was born with the name Campbell: Argyll Street, Campbell Road and Lorne Court were named for them. The House of Windsor is represented by Elizabeth Street, Anne Street, Charles Street, George Street, and Crown Street.

COSGROVE

A name recorded as Covesgrave in 1086 and Couesgraua in 1167. A Saxon personal name and suffix *graf*, meaning 'the grove of a man called Cof'.

Locally is Isworth, a name describing 'Hycgi's *worth* or enclosure'; this is a pallisade of logs or poles designed to keep livestock in the settlement overnight rather than a defensive feature against the highly unlikely possibility of an attack.

COTON

Domesday's record of 1086 gives the name as simply Cote, although a little over a century later, in 1195, it is Cotes. The modern name is derived from Old English *cot*, or more accurately, the plural *cotum*, and speaks of the '(place at) the cottages'. The difference between Domesday's record and later forms may appear to indicate it is singular; however, there is no reason to assume this, and in truth, the listing of the name in the great work is most likely inaccurate.

COTTERSTOCK

This name shows several similar forms over a period of two centuries, beginning with Codestoche in 1086, through Codestoc in 1125, Cothestoche in 1175, and Cotherstoke in 1254, to Cotherstock in 1275. Despite this collection of names, it is difficult to give the origin with any certainty; indeed, there are four quite plausible meanings for this place name.

First came the suggestion that it showed the Old English elements *cothe*, used to suggest 'sickness or pestilence', and *stoc*, which is 'special place'. In combination, it is understood to refer to 'a hospital', yet there is no record of such being here. Furthermore, the hospital would not have been here prior to the settlement being founded and we would expect to find the name of the place as well as the reference to a hospital.

Next is the Old English *cother-stoc*, the definition of which depends upon how the suffix is interpreted as being particularly 'special'. The prefix is used to denote a gathering of some description and a definition has been suggested of 'dairy farm'. However, there must be some doubt as to the accuracy of this definition, for normally the term for a specialised farm is *wic* and in almost every case this was a dairy farm.

Thus, the third alternative takes the same Old English term, *cother-stoc*, but gives a different interpretation. Consider the two elements here meaning 'gathering' and 'special place'. Together they could well indicate a meeting place, a venue for a gathering of the local officials and representatives to discuss legal matters.

Last there is the old favourite of reverting to a personal name. There are a number of well-known names which would fit this evidence reasonably well, yet it is often too tempting to suggest the name of an individual when that element is proving troublesome. Further evidence dating from before Domesday's record would be ideal; however, this does not seem likely and the meaning of the name will, therefore, remain uncertain.

COTTESBROOK

A name recorded in 1086 as Cotesbroc and in 1220 as Cottesbroc, which is derived from a Saxon personal name with the Old English *broc*. Despite the similarity with the previous names, there is no doubt this describes 'Cott's brook'.

Mitley Spinney is a small area of woodland which is named after 'the middle hill' which gave it a name. Calender Farm is thought to be derived from Kaylend, a place given to the abbot and convent of Sulby, who placed a small cell here, and thus the name was transferred here. However, the name of Kaylend has never been understood.

COTTINGHAM

With records of Cotingeham in 1086, Cotingham in 1137, and Cottingeham in 1163, this is of Old English derivation. Here, a personal name is followed by the elements *inga* and *ham*, giving the homestead of the family or followers of a man called Cott (or Cotta)'.

Great Cattage Wood refers to 'the wild cat hedge', but there is little evidence that this rare animal would ever have been found here, for the habitat is simply not typical wild cat country. Hence, the likelihood is this is being used as a nickname, perhaps even a derogatory term for someone who lived here.

COURTEENHALL

A very unusual name, mainly because it has evolved little since the thirteenth century. The earliest record we have is from 1086 as Cortenhale, with Curtehala in 1110, and Cortenhal in 1196. This Saxon name features the suffix *halh* and speaks of 'Corta or Curta's nook of land'.

CRANFORD ST ANDREW

The basic name here comes from the Old English *cran-ford*, telling us it was 'the ford where cranes (or heron) are seen'. Recorded in 1086 as Craneford, the first addition is seen in 1254 as Craneford Sancti Andree, a name which refers to the dedication of the local church.

CRANFORD ST JOHN

As with the previous name, this is 'the ford of the cranes or heron'. The name is recorded in 1167 as Cranford, the addition first seen in 1254 as Craneford Sancti Iohannis and, once again, taken from the local church.

The station here is the last remaining evidence of the former Kettering Ironstone Railway. This narrow gauge industrial transport system served the ironstone works on a three-mile circuit from the 1870s until 1962.

CREATON

An ancient name which originates in the landscape. The earliest written record of the place is from the eleventh century as Cretone, Creptone, and Craptone, with Creton in 1197, and Creiton in 1202. Here, two languages combine to form the name: Celtic *creig* is suffixed by Old English *tun*, giving 'the farmstead at the rock or cliff'.

CRICK

As with the previous name, an ancient name indeed, derived from the Celtic tongue spoken since before the Roman-British era. However, the earliest record of the place is from 1086 as Crec, later Kreic in 1201, and Creck in 1254. This can be seen to be related to Old Welsh *creic* and the Celtic or British *cruc* and mean '(the place at) the rock or cliff'.

The name of Crack's Hill was known as Crick Hill until at least 1839, thus was the original place name. Flavell's Lodge is named after the family of Andrew Flavel of Kilsby, who were associated with this place by 1621.

The Red Lion Inn shows the symbol which originally referred to John of Gaunt and later to Scotland following the Act of Union in 1707.

CROUGHTON

There are many examples of this name to peruse – Creveltone, Criweltone, Crouelton, Craulton, Crewelton and Croulton dating from the eleventh to the beginning of the thirteenth century. Here is an Old English or Saxon name derived from *creowel-tun* or 'the farmstead on the fork of land'.

Rowler's Farm is found on the 'rough hill' which gave it the name derived from Old English *ruh hlaw*. The Blackbird Inn takes advantage of one of the most common birds in the land and, because of its colour, one of the easiest to represent.

CULWORTH

In 1086, it is Culeorde, in 1195, Culwurthe, in 1230, Culwurth, and in 1254, Culwrth. Another Saxon name, here with the suffix *worth*, telling us this was 'Cula's enclosure'.

D'Anvers House recalls this estate was held by the Danvers family from the fifteenth century. Wadground Barn may not have stored the plant, yet the place was formerly where woad was grown. The plant is native to south-eastern Europe but was cultivated here from ancient times; indeed, it was probably brought to these shores when the first farmers arrived. It is famed for being used as a dye with which they adorned their bodies; indeed, the northern tribes of Britain were known as Picts (or Picti) by the Romans, which refers to them as 'painted ones' in Latin. However, the plant was still used up to the sixteenth century as the only source of blue dye, while the Lindisfarne Gospels show it was also used as a pigment for their illustrations.

Chapter 4

Daventry–Duston

DAVENTRY

In Domesday, this name is recorded as Daventrei, and in 1150 as Dauintre. This is an Old English name derived from a personal name followed by *treow* and giving us '(place at) the tree of a man called Dafa'.

Borough Hill marks the position of 'the old fortification'; Burntwalls Farm was once known for having 'burned or ruined walls'; Middlemoor Farm is a corruption of *micel mor*, 'the big marsh'; and Stepnell Spinney took its name from 'the steep hill'. The name of Hackwood Farm tells us this was 'the hacked wood' and tells us it had been felled or chopped regularly. Fousill Wood is derived from Old English *fugol wielle* and tells us it was 'the bird's spring or stream', one where birds flocked again and again; Drayton is a common place name which we should expect to have a second element were it larger – the name always comes from *draeg tun*, a portage where a load or cargo was dragged overland to avoid a barrier in a river, to cross from one water course to another, or to cross a difficult part of a road; and finally, Falconershill is named after John Fawckener, whose family were here by 1621.

Pubs here include the Fleur de Lys, the heraldic representation of France; the Plume of Feathers features an image of the three ostrich feathers which represent the Prince of Wales; the Saracens Head is another heraldic image, showing that a member of that family fought in the Crusades; the Falconer is another easily recognised symbol, one which may also have been another service provided by the innkeeper; the Pike and Eel is a clear fishing reference; the Dun Cow Inn refers to the colour, a brown cow and a common rural sight; the Romer Arms was renamed such by former owner Romer Williams, a former lawyer who was renowned for his love of hunting.

One theme chosen for the streets here is that of soldiers, not individuals but specific kinds of fighting units. Off Yeomanry Way, which speaks of a group formed to protect or guard, as in the Yeomen of the Guard, is Grenadier Road, named for the soliders originally used for assualt operations and derived from their use of grenade-like weapons; Cavalry Drive refers to those who are mounted on horses and is derived from the French *cheval* meaning 'horse'; Fusilier Road refers to those who were armed with a light musket known as a fusil; and Coldstream Close, after the Coldstream Guards, the oldest continuously serving regiment of the British Army who take their name from Coldstream in Scotland.

DEENE

Found as just Den in 1065, Dene in 1086 and Dena in 1163, this is undoubtedly from the Saxon *denu*, meaning 'valley'.

DEENETHORPE

A place and a name closely linked to the previous entry. Domesday shows it as simply Torp, with a single later entry of Denetorp in 1169. The element *thorp* is Old Scandinavian and refers to an outlying settlement, undoubtedly one which was earlier an offshoot of the previous place.

DENFORD

There is more than a little similarity with the previous names here: the first element is the same. Listed as Deneforde in 1086 and Deneford in 1195, this tells us this was the '(place at) the ford in the valley'.

The Cock Inn is often given as being an indication that cock fighting took place here. However, since the seventeenth century, it was also an advertisement for cock ale: boiled and minced meat of a cockerel, producing a jelly, which is mixed with ale and 'other ingredients'.

DENTON

Unlike the previous names, and every other place of this name in the country, the first element is not Old English *denu*. Records of this name are as *Dodintone* in 1086, Dudinton in 1200, and Parva Dudinton in 1220. Here, the personal name is followed by the elements *inga* and *tun*, which gives 'the farmstead of the family or followers of Dodda (or Dudda)'.

DESBOROUGH

Records of this name from the eleventh to the thirteenth centuries are plentiful. We find Desburg, Dereburg, Deresburc, Deresburg, and Desburc, all of which show this to be 'the stronghold of a man called Deor'. This Old English or Saxon place name finds the suffix *burh* preceded by a personal name, which is probably a nickname, for it is also the word used to mean 'deer' or more generally 'animal'. As a name, the latter 'animal' is the more likely definition, used in a complimentary sense to describe a trait usually attributed to an animal. That it is clearly a nickname is obvious, for at birth, no parent would name their son 'animal'!

Locals enjoy a drink at the Oak Tree, a reminder that large or unusual trees were markers pointing out the pub from afar.

DINGLEY

Records of this name are found as Dinglei in 1086, Dingelea in 1175, and as Dingelai in 1197. Here is another example of a hybrid name, although not from separate cultures but different eras. Old English evolved into Middle English; the time frame is difficult to tie down, for use of the earlier tongue would have lingered in some regions much the same as speakers of Cornish (and no other tongue) existed until the middle of the twentieth century. Here, the later *dingle* has preceded the earlier common suffix of *leah*, telling us of 'the woodland clearing with hollows'.

DODFORD

Three possible origins for this name, depending upon the interpretation. Records have been found of Doddanford in 792 and Dodeforde in 1086, which has led to the definition of a Saxon name telling us this was 'Dodda's ford'. However, there is also a plant known as dod, common to the waterside along the Nene and which would certainly have grown alongside the margins of the ford.

A third possibility depends upon when the ford was first used. In the book *Salt Routes*, this author walked as closely as possible to the ancient trackways set out between the small settlements. Among the longest-lived markers in the landscape are the ancient river crossings, although in the modern era, there is invariably a bridge near that point. Those who marked out these trackways were known as dodmen or dodders and were highly respected by their fellow men. Undoubtedly, there must have been some places which were named after these individuals and Dodford may well be one.

DRAUGHTON

Here we see an element which is never found alone but always in combination. This is the Old Scandinavian *drag*, derived from the same Indo-European language root as Old English *draeg* and with the same meaning. However, the differences in pronunciation have meant a slight variation in the place names, the Old English *draeg* appearing as Dray- today.

The name of Draughton comes from *drag* with the addition of Old English *tun*; such hybrid names are common in regions where the two cultures had influence during the pre-Norman era. Together, the two single-syllable words from two cultures bring forth an image of life in the area when the name was first coined. The name of Draughton tells us it was 'the farmstead on a slope used for the dragging of timbers (and likely other large items too)'. Today, the place would be described as a lumber yard, working wood to form smaller more manageable pieces and probably to order.

DUDDINGTON

Listed as Dodintone in 1086, Duditun in 1156, and Duditon in 1206, here we find a personal name with the Old English elements *ing* and *tun*. This can be defined as 'the estate of Dudda or Dodda's people'.

DUNCOTE

In 1276, this name appears as Doncote and forty years later as Donecote. This is an Old English name featuring the element *cot* and meaning 'Dunna's cottage(s)'.

DUSTON

Very little difference in the records of this name. Domesday shows it as Dustone and the modern form appears as early as 1178. Such similar forms are a hindrance to defining the name; however, the name is simple enough to enable us to give two equally plausible alternatives for this name, both of which are Old English. This is either *dus-tun* 'the farmstead on a mound', or *dust tun* 'the farmstead on dusty soil'. Without further examples, the name will probably never be understood.

Local pubs include the Melbourne Arms, named after William Lamb, the 2nd Viscount Melbourne (1779-1848), who schooled the young Queen Victoria in the affairs of state. His title was taken from Melbourne in Derbyshire and from him given to Melbourne in Australia, itself thought previously to be known as Doutta-galla, said to be either the name of a respected tribal elder or perhaps meaning 'treeless plain'. In the nineteenth century, Melbourne was one of the great scandal stories of the day, for his wife was novelist Lady Caroline Lamb and, of more interest to the public, lover of the poet Lord Byron.

Other pubs include the Longboat, a reference to the nearby canal system; the Rifle Butt, probably a reminder of a former landlord's earlier life; and Squirrels shows the image of one of the most easily recognised of animals.

Chapter 5

Earls Barton–Eye

EARLS BARTON

Records of this name are few but distinctly different – in 1086, it is simply Bartone, in 1187, Barton Comitis David, and by 1290, the modern form is first seen. The basic name is a common one, always from Old English *bere tun* 'barley farm', although some sources do suggest *baer tun*, meaning 'corn store in the outlying grange', as an alternative.

As with many common place names, there has been an addition for distinction, here telling of the lands being held by the Earl of Huntingdon. For a short time, as evidenced from the twelfth-century listing, this region was held or managed by a friend or colleague named David.

When looking at the history of pub signs, it is clear that imagery is more important than the name; this is to be expected as, for much of the life of pubs, most potential customers were illiterate. This imagery conveyed the simplest of meanings: the Old Swan suggests grace and elegance, the Stags Head strength, and the Boot Inn the military.

EAST CARLTON

Carlton is a common place name also seen as Carleton and even Charlton. Clearly, with so many differing modern forms, the origin must have been quite simple. Indeed, those few differences are a result of the region's influence by both Saxon and Scandinavian cultures. The meaning in all cases is the same.

Domesday records the name as Carlintone in 1086, and there is a Carleton in 1199. Here, the suffix is Old English *tun*, meaning 'farmstead', and preceded by the telling reference. In the three examples given, the two elements of note here are the Old English *ceorl* and the Old Scandinavian *karla*, both having a common root and both referring to a 'freeman' or 'villein'. The gentleman in question was once a serf and is now a freeman and this place was once where he settled down to an agricultural existence. It would be interesting to know the story of how he earned his freedom, unlike the addition, which simply describes the location near to Carlton Curlieu in neighbouring Leicestershire.

EAST FARNDON

A name recorded as Ferendone, Faredone, Ferendon and Farendon in the eleventh and twelfth centuries. The basic name comes from the Old English *fearn dun* or '(place at) the hill where ferns grow'. The addition is to differentiate with West Farndon.

Easton Maudit church of St Peter and St Paul.

To the west of the village is a large stone known as the Judith Stone. Deposited by a glacier as the ice receded at the end of the last ice age, it was likely used as a boundary marker at some stage and most likely named after Countess Judith, niece of William the Conqueror, who held this manor at the time of Domesday.

EAST HADDON

This place is listed as Eddone, Hadone, Haddon and Esthaddon between the end of the eleventh and beginning of the thirteenth centuries. This is from the Old English or Saxon *haeth dun*, meaning '(place at) the hill where heather grows', with the addition to differentiate from West Haddon, less than four miles away.

EASTON MAUDIT

Domesday lists this place as Estone in 1086 and Estonemaudeut in 1298. A common name of Saxon origins which comes from the Old English elements *east* and *tun*, predictably 'the eastern farmstead'. Such common place names often come with an addition. Here, it is the Mauduit family, here from the twelfth century.

A welcome to Easton Maudit.

EASTON NESTON

Found in Domesday as Estanestone and also Adestanestone, this is an unusual name, for there is no actual addition in the normal sense. Over the centuries, what had begun life as 'Aedstan's *tun* or farmstead' has been thought to be two words and that is how it appears today.

Locally, we find Hulcote, a rather uncomplimentary name describing 'the hovel-like cottages'. Clearly nobody would describe their home as a hovel – to them it was simply 'home' – hence it is further evidence that place names were rarely coined by those who lived there but by the neighbouring settlements. Nun Wood was a possession of the nearby nuns of Sewardsley, and Sewardsley itself described 'Sigeweard's woodland clearing'.

EASTON-ON-THE-HILL

Few records of this name still exist and none with the addition until comparatively recently. However, we can still define this common name, hence the addition, for little has changed over the centuries. As with the previous entry, this name is from the Old English *east tun*, 'the eastern farmstead', with the addition also having an obvious meaning.

Here too is Easton Hornstocks, which takes the name of the place and adds a description of an oddly-shaped tree stump. Vigo Lodge is named after the victory by the Anglo-Dutch vessels commanded by Admiral George Rooke over the French and Spanish fleet at Vigo Bay in 1702. The allies had been seeking to establish a maritime base on the Iberian Peninsula, when news came through of Spanish ships returning from the New World carrying silver and other treasures. These ships were protected by a French escort and had entered the bay when attacked by the Anglo-Dutch. Every French vessel was destroyed and the Spanish either met a similar fate or were captured. Such place names were common when celebrating a famous victory.

ECTON

There are three forms of note for this name, *Echentone* in 1086, *Echeton* in 1165, and *Eketon* in 1221. Here, a Saxon personal name precedes the most common suffix in English place names in *tun*, giving us 'the farmstead of a man called Ecca'.

Where the Three Horseshoes Inn now stands was once, as the name suggests, the village blacksmith. For three centuries, the ancestors of one of the USA's most famous historical figures shod countless horses, for here was the family of Benjamin Franklin.

EDGCOTE

Found in Domesday as Hocecote, as Hochecote in 1159, and as Echecott in 1223, this name features Old English suffix *cot* meaning 'cottages'. The first element here is a reference to the Hwicce, the name of a tribe, although perhaps it should be understood as referring to a member of that tribe as in 'the cottages of the Hwiccian'.

Local names include Paddle Cottage, a name from *pad wella* meaning 'the spring noted for its toads'.

ELKINGTON

Found as Eltetone in Domesday, as Heltedun in 1200, and as Eltindon in 1283. This may well be a Saxon personal name and thus the '(place near) Elta's *dun* or hill slope'; however, there is a possibility that this is Old English *elfetu* or 'swan'.

Locally, we see Honey Hill, a name which has no connection to the most natural of foods. This is from Old English *han*, meaning 'stone, rock', and thus describing 'the very stony hill'.

ETTON

Listed as Etona in 1125 and as Ecton in 1189, this place was always a part of Northamptonshire until border changes in the late twentieth century. This is from Old English and describes 'Eata's farmstead'.

Local names include Simon's Wood, a modern representation of the original 'Sigemund's wood'.

EVENLEY

The records of this name are limited to Evelai and Avelai in 1086, Euenlai in 1147, and Evenle in 1226. This name is comprised of two Old English elements, *efen* and *leah*, meaning '(place at) the even (flat) woodland clearing'.

Locally, we find Plowman's Furze, named after the family of John le Plomer who were here by 1381.

EVERDON

We find the earliest record dated 944 as Eferdun, with Eofordunenga gemaere in 1021, and Everdone in 1086. The middle of these three has a second element meaning 'great' and there are two settlements today – this one and a Little Everdon – with less than a kilometre between them. The tenth-century record is the closest to the original Old English *eofor dun*, meaning '(place at) the hill frequented by wild boars'.

Minor place names here include Snorscomb, which may seem to come from Old English *snoc* meaning 'the projection, or point', but there is no such feature here, and so this is probably a personal name and thus 'Snoc's valley'. Hen Wood is much easier to see, for it has changed little since 'the wood where female birds are found'.

Everdon's local pub is the Plough, a simple image which is one of the most common names and also one of the oldest. Today, the image is a painted sign; in the earliest days, it was probably an old ploughshare.

EYDON

Six miles south of here is the village of Aynho, which, as we saw under that listing, refers to the personal name Aega. Here we find the same personal name with the suffix *dun*, giving 'Aega's hill'. The spelling reflected the pronunciation for most of its history; it is only very recently that we have attempted to pronounce the name as it is written, for until quite recently, most of the nation was illiterate and spelling was entirely reliant on the person recording the details. Historically, the name has been found as Egedone in 1086, Eindon in 1202, and Eyndon and Eydon in 1254.

The local is the Royal Oak, the most popular 'royal' name and referring to the escape of King Charles II in 1651.

EYE

What was a part of Northamptonshire, officially known as the Soke of Peterborough, this is recorded as Ege in 970, Ege in 972, and Aya in 1199. This is from Old English *eg* and is the ancestor of the modern world 'island' but was used by the Saxons to describe any drier land in a wetter area, even that which was seasonal.

Local names include Singlesole Farm, which tells us it was 'Singulf's woodland', and Tanholt House was built on the region described as *raenel holt* or 'where wicker baskets are made'.

Chapter 6

Far Cotton–Furtho

FAR COTTON

The only record of any age is from 1196 as simply Cotes. There is no doubt this is from a plural of Old English *cot* telling us of 'the cottages'. The addition of Far is one of obvious meaning and distinguishes it from similarly named places. Furthermore, it seems to have been a quite recent addition.

There is a St Leonard's Road here, named after the hospice and associated chapel south of the river, which catered for lepers.

In 1863, on 17 April, Walter Dew entered this world in this quiet village as one of seven children born to railway guard Walter Snr and Eliza. The family moved to London ten years afterwards, where the young Walter found work in a solicitor's office, then as a clerk for a seed merchant, then in 1881, he was listed in the Census as a railway porter.

However, it was the next year when he entered the police force and rose through the ranks to write his name into criminal history, not once but twice. As a detective constable in the CID at Whitechapel, he was to find himself one of those in the search for the notorious Jack the Ripper in 1888. His memoirs, published in 1938, do conflict with the official records and he seems to have stretched several points so as to involve himself.

Later, in 1910, now Inspector Dew was certainly pivotal in the investigation and eventual arrest of the infamous Dr Crippen. The murderer's arrest is known for being the first to use wireless to lead to an arrest. Crippen, travelling aboard the much slower SS *Montrose*, was overtaken by the SS *Laurentic* and he was arrested by Dew who had boarded disguised as a pilot officer.

FARTHINGHOE

A name which is listed as Ferningeho in 1086, Ferninghou in 1196, Farningho in 1220, and Fernighou in 1239. There is some uncertainty as to the origins of this unusual place name, yet it is most likely to be found as '(the place at) the hill spur of the people among the ferns'. The Old English *fearn inga hoh* would then be the beginnings of the name.

A glance at a map of this place will show it to be on a grid system and is an example of a medieval town planned in exquisite detail, rather than the haphazard collection of dwellings normally associated with villages of the period. Furthermore, the local pronunciation is still similar to the thirteenth century forms and is not unlike 'farnigo'.

The Fox Inn is another easily recognised symbol; the creature is found throughout the land and seen as crafty, stylish, indeed it epitomises the lovable rogue.

Farthinghoe church of St Michael and
All Angels.

FARTHINGSTONE

The similarity between this and the previous place name is purely coincidental; the origins are quite different. Here the name is a hybrid between and Old Scandinavian personal name and the Old English suffix *tun*, giving us 'the farmstead of a man called Farthegn'. Early forms of this name are many but ostensibly the same, being found as Fordinestone in 1086, Fardingestun in 1167, Fardeneston in 1177, Fordingeston in 1184, Ferdingestone in 1232 and Farthingeston in 1261. The confusion with 'ford' and 'stone' is common and likely to be found in many such names.

Local names include Castle Dykes, a hill which still shows its ancient trenches despite being overgrown with trees and underbrush. Two former familes are remembered in other names: Knightley Wood tells how the Knightley family held this manor by at least 1535, while Mantles Heath was owned by the family of John Mauntel.

The Kings Arms is a popular sign, showing support for both king and country generally, rather than a particular monarch.

FAWSLEY

With records as Fealuwes lea in 944, Faleuuesle in 1086, Fealeweslea in 1110, Faleslea in 1167, and Faleweslea in 1190, this name has posed some problems. The idea of this first element being a personal name derived from *fealu* is difficult to see, hence this must be *fealu leah* 'the fallow-coloured woodland clearing' or, more likely, the 'woodland clearing frequented by fallow deer'.

Minor names found here include Sewell's Pond, which does seem like a personal name but is actually derived from the 'seven springs' which feed it.

Finedon's town sign.

Finedon's largest building.

FINEDON

The tendency for 'f' to replace 'th', especially at the beginning of words, is not confined to the modern era. Old records of this name appear as Tingdene in 1086, Thingdene in 1200, and Thingden in 1230; the change to the 'f' is very recent, probably in use from around the eighteenth century. This name comes from Old English *thing denu*, which tells us this was 'the valley where assemblies are held'.

The Bell Inn claims to be the oldest licensed site in England and to have stood here since before Domesday. However, the present building is not eleventh century, and there is good evidence to suggest the earlier building was a couple of hundred yards away and there is no knowing how old this was.

The vast majority of pubs named the Prince of Wales refer to the future Edward VII, eldest son of Queen Victoria, who was known as such from 1862 to 1901, one of the longest to hold this office. The Dolben Arms remembers the family who purchased estates here in the seventeenth century and who are remembered for their musical and religious careers.

FLORE

Domesday's record is just the same as the modern form, which is not greatly helpful in defining the name. It seems highly likely that the origin is Old English or Saxon *flor*, which means what it says: 'floor'. As we know the meaning, we need to ascertain how

Flore's attractive village sign.

the term is used here. Obviously, the 'floor' must have been quite exceptional, which is the best clue we have. The best-known 'floors' of the time were remnants from the days of the Roman occupation, thus it must refer to a tessellated floor or pavement and point to a site of Roman occupation.

The name of Glassthorpe Hill refers to the '*thorp* or outlying farmstead of a man called Klak'. This origin can be seen in two places in Sweden, both called Klastorp.

The White Hart is a pub name which, if it is heraldic, can be traced back to Richard III. However, some time during the nineteenth or twentieth centuries, it became the generic name for an inn or tavern, much the same as a vacuum cleaner has become a 'hoover' irrespective of the manufacturer.

FOTHERINGHAY

There are a number of records worthy of note here, as Frodigeia in 1086, Fodringeia in 1163, Foddringeia in 1176, and Fodringeie in 1201. All point to a likely origin of *fodring eg*, a Saxon term describing 'the island or well-irrigated land used for grazing'. The term 'island' is used historically to describe a dry area in land which is almost permanently wet or marshy, not in the same sense as today.

FURTHO

Listed as Forho in Domesday, as Fordho in 1220, and as Fortho in 1254, this name is derived from Old English *ford hoh* and describes 'the ford by the spur of land'. The Watling Street was the road in question.

Knotwood Farm speaks of the *hnott wudu* 'the bald or close cut wood', and thus referring to a pollarded and well-managed woodland.

Chapter 7

Gayton–Guilsborough

GAYTON

A place recorded as Gaiton in 1163, as Gainton in 1167, and as Gauton in 1196, which shows the name comes from a different source to most places so-named. The majority have the first element from Old Scandinavian *geit* meaning 'goat'. However, this example is a Saxon name telling us of the 'Gaga's farmstead', with the common suffix *tun*.

One gentleman who took his name from this place was Sir Philip de Gayton, one of the family whose tombs can be found in the village church, and a man who had two daughters whose deeds are a part of folklore. One, named Scholastica, is remembered for having murdered her husband, a crime for which she apparently did not pay. Her sister Julianna, who had a daughter, Mabila, was later 'found' to be a witch and, unlike her sister, paid for the accusation with her life, burned at the stake as was the punishment of the day.

GEDDINGTON

Here we have a name which combines a Scandinavian or Saxon personal name with Saxon elements to produce 'the estate of a man called Gaete or Geiti'. The Old English elements here are *ing* and *tun*, which is revealed by an expert eye being cast over records such as Geitentone in 1086, Gadintona in 1130, Gaitintun in 1157, Gatinton in 1159, and Gattinton in 1163.

The local name of Sart Wood is derived from what can only be described as an Anglo-French term, *sart* meaning 'a woodland clearing'. The names of Great Brand and Little Brand tell us this was land 'cleared by burning'.

Two pubs here are named after coloured animals: the White Hart is ultimately a reference to Richard III and the White Lion could be referring to Edward IV, the earls of March, or here possibly the dukes of Norfolk.

In 1290, Edward I led the funeral procession of his wife Eleanor of Castile, on the journey to Westminster Abbey. The slow procession stopped overnight several time on the route from near Lincoln, including here at Geddington. Four years later, a succession of twelve monuments were erected marking the resting places of the queen, only three remain, of which the best is undoubtedly found here.

GLAPTHORN

Few different forms of this name are recorded; indeed, only two have been found of note – as Glapethorn in 1189, and as Glapthorn from 1202. There can be no doubt this comes from the Old English *thorn* preceded by a personal name, giving '(the place at) Glappa's thorn tree'.

Provost Lodge was a manor which endowed a provost and twelve chaplains of the Church of St Andrew at Cotterstock.

GLENDON

Records of Clendone, Clenedune, Clendon and Glendon between the eleventh and thirteenth centuries show this is from Old English *claenan dun* and is found 'at the clean hill'.

Brookside Spinney is of obvious origins; however, the name may have been different today had the family of the thirteenth-century tenant Robert Bithebrook (by the brook) remained here for long.

GRAFTON REGIS

The basic name here is more common than would be thought, with approximately ten examples of major places of this name in England. With one notable exception, all these have the same origins in 'farmstead by a grove', taken from the Old English *graf tun*. The addition is, somewhat predictably, a reference to this being the 'king's land' and is recorded as the same from the twelfth century.

GRAFTON UNDERWOOD

As with the previous name, this is 'the farmstead by a grove'. Listed as Grastone in 1086 and Grafton in 1202, the addition is first seen in 1367 as Grafton Underwode. This is a name meaning 'under or near the wood' and a reference to Rockingham Forest.

The former RAF airfield was assigned to the United States Army Eighth Air Force in 1942. A granite memorial on the edge of the airfield marks the deaths of 1,579 US airmen who died in the Second World War while serving here.

GREAT ADDINGTON

A name recorded just as Edintone in 1086, Edintona in 1130, and as Maior Adinton in 1220. This is of Old English derivation from a Saxon personal name followed by *ing-tun* and speaking of 'the estate associated with a man called Eadda or Aeddi'.

Shooters Hill has been suggested as being where archery target practice was held; however, this would be an unusual definition, for such names usually refer to a muddy slope.

The Hare & Hounds public house is a flashback to the days of hare hunting using hounds, most often beagles. This is different from hare coursing, which uses greyhounds, although neither had a particularly succesful capture rate.

GREAT BILLING

Listed in Domesday as Bellinge, in 1206 as Billinnge Magna, and in 1223 as Billinges, this Saxon personal name is followed by the element *ingas*. Together, they tell us this was once '(the place of) the family or followers of a man called Bill or Billa'. Predictably, the addition was given to differentiate between the two settlements, which are quite near each other.

The Elwes Arms public house and Elwes Way are both named after Gervase Elwes (1866-1921), an English tenor who was born Gervase Henry Cary-Elwes. His career ended abruptly when he was involved in a rail accident in Boston, Massachusetts. Trying to retrieve an overcoat, he fell from the platform and was hit by the train as his wife watched from a short distance. We also find Lady Winefride's Walk, named after his wife Lady Winifrede Fielding, daughter of the Earl of Denbigh. Valentine Way was named after Mr Valentine Cary-Elwes.

GREAT BRINGTON

Domesday lists this as both Brinintone and Brintone in 1086, with later records of Brinton in 1198, and Brunton in 1248. This name is of Old English beginnings and is 'the estate associated with a man called Bryni' and sees the personal name suffixed by the elements *ing* and *tun*. The addition is to differentiate with the smaller settlement less than a mile north of here and most likely an overspill created when some of the farming community required extra storage and/or grazing areas.

Local names include Gaburrow Hill, meaning 'the cold hill'; Nobottle is 'the new building'; Chinkwell Clumps refers to a spring which bubbles through from a chink in the ground; and Washington's House was a name brought here by Lawrence Washington of Sulgrave in 1616.

Great Brington was once mentioned in the *Guiness Book of World Records* as the birthplace of Betsy Russell Baker. Having emigrated to Nebraska, USA, she died on 24 October 1955, exactly 113 years and sixty-five days after her birth, making her the longest-lived (proven) human being in history at that time. She held this record, albeit posthumously, until 1959.

GREAT CRANSLEY

A name found twice within half a mile, hence the addition of Great, although the region of Broughton known as Little Cransley has been developed and the population is today noticeably larger. This comes from the Old English *cran-leah* or '(the place at) the woodland clearing frequented by cranes or herons'. It is recorded as Cranslea bricg in 956, Craneslea in 1086, and Cranesleia in 1202.

The meaning of the place name was not lost on those who named the local pub, which is known as the Three Cranes.

GREAT DODDINGTON

First seen as Dudinton in 1174 and later as Magna Dodington in 1309. Here we find a Saxon personal name followed by the Old English elements *ing* and *tun*, telling us this was 'the estate associated with a man called either Dudda or Dodda'. The smaller version of the place, Little Doddington, was to the south of here.

The Stags Head is popular as a pub name, for it represents strength and is easily recognised. The stag is almost always a male red deer in its prime at around five years.

GREAT HARROWDEN

This name, as well as its namesake less than a mile away, is listed as Hargindone in 1086, Harhgeduna in 1155, Harewedon in 1202, and Maior Harewedon in 1220. This is from the Old English *hearg* and *dun*, speaking of 'the hill where the temple or shrine is found'. Clearly, these would have been from the pre-Christian era, while it is a pity that the name of the god or gods worshipped here is unknown, for it would have revealed a lot more about the people who first settled here.

Frisby Lodge was home to Robert Paige of Friseby, who lived here in 1282. The record of this man has been uncovered from a rather unusual source. Robert Paige was sheriff of Northamptonshire and, in a document of 1282, was ordered to deliver a Northampton prisoner named Robert de Harewedon to Worcester, where six men would be on hand to take custody of him and bring him before the King on Whitsunday of that year.

GREAT HOUGHTON

The basic name is very common, found throughout England. Invariably, as with this one, it comes from Old English *hoh-tun* or 'the farmstead on or by a ridge'. Records of the name are limited to Hohtone in 1086 and Magna Houtona in 1199.

Plaxwell's Barn is a corruption of a personal name and *wiella*, and thus either Saxon 'Clacc's spring or stream' or Old Norse 'Klak's spring or stream'.

GREAT OXENDON

Today, there is no place called Little Oxendon, the smaller medieval village was abandoned years ago and no trace remains, the name of Great Oxendon being one of the few clues, although there are some traces in the landscape. The differences between the two are obvious.

The basic name is recorded as Oxendone in 1086, Oxendon in 1176, and Maior Oxendon in 1220. It is derived from the Old English *oxa* (in a plural form) with *dun* and giving us '(place at) the hill where oxen are allowed to graze'.

GREATWORTH

In 1086, this name is recorded as Grentevorde, in 1200 as Gretteworth, in 1206 as Gretewrd, and in 1254 as Gruttewrth. This name comes from the Old English *greot worth* meaning '(the place at) the gravelly enclosure'.

The name of Cockleyhill Farm is derived from Old English *cock hlaw hyll* or the 'male bird hill, hill'.

GREENS NORTON

Norton is one of the most common place names in the country, which is why there is an addition for distinction. As with all the other so-named places, this comes from the Old English *north tun* 'the northern farmstead' and is obviously named by a settlement to the south, although which is unknown. A place recorded in Domesday as Nortone in 1086, and as Grenesnorton, with a name which we would expect to find as Norton Green if it referred to the village green. However, the Greens shows a possessive 's' which points to a manorial name, which is found in records dating from the fourteenth century, when the Grene family were in residence.

Here is Caswell, which tells us it was 'the spring or stream where cress grew', and Duncot is from 'Dunna's cottages'.

Early innkeepers would often perform two services for the community, more often than most that of butcher and hence the Butcher's Arms here.

The village of Greens Norton.

The half moon at Grendon.

GRENDON

A name found several times in the counties around central England, as here, usually from the Old English *grene dun*, the '(place at) the green hill'. It is recorded as Grendone in 1086 and as the modern form as early as 1186.

GRETTON

Here we find a place name also seen in Gloucestershire and Shropshire. However, each has a somewhat different origin. In Northamptonshire, the name comes from the Old English *greot tun*, speaking of the 'farmstead on or by gravel'. It is recorded as Gretone in 1086 and exactly as the modern form in 1163.

Kirby Hall is the sole reminder of the 'church and the village' from Old Scandinavian *kirkja by*, for neither the place of worship nor the settlement have been here for many years. Thatchams Copse tells us this was where 'reeds for thatching were gathered in the water meadow'.

Three pubs here with three quite different origins. The Blue Bell Inn may conjure up images of the spring flower, yet this is a reminder of the church, the colour being associated with Christianity. The Talbot Inn is named after the white hunting dog with black spots, a variety of hound noted for its remarkable olfactory sense. Thirdly, the Hatton Arms, thought to be the second oldest pub in the county with parts dating back to the fourteenth century, is named from the seventeenth-century lord of the manor, Sir Christopher Hatton, then serving as Elizabeth I's Lord Chamberlain. However, at the time, this place was known as the Lord's Arms and was run by James Chappel, the former servant of Sir Christopher who had saved him and his family from an explosion on the island of Guernsey. As a mark of his gratitude, Chappel was granted a healthy pension on top of almost certainly becoming the first black landlord in the land.

Guilsborough village sign.

GRIMSCOTE

A name found recorded as Grimescot in 1199, which points to a meaning of 'cottages belonging to a man called Grimr'. This comes from the Old Scandinavian personal name suffixed by the Old English *cot*.

GUILSBOROUGH

Recorded as Gildesburgh in 1066, as Gisleburg in 1225, and as Gildesburc in 1225, here is a name of Old English or Saxon origin featuring a personal name with the element *burh*. Here we are told this was once the 'stronghold of a man called Gyldi'.

Nortoft Grange is an Old Scandinavian name referring to 'the northern homestead', and Lindow Spinney stands on the *lind hoh* or 'lime tree hill'. The local here is the Ward Arms, lords of this manor since John Ward purchased this manor from the Belcher family in 1710.

Mother and daughter Agnes Brown and Joan Vaughan were local women who, along with two other women and a man, were hanged on 22 July 1612 for the crime of witchcraft. They were accused of bewitching a local noblewoman of the manor house, Elizabeth Belcher, and her sister's husband, Master Avery. Also, their crimes included killing a child and many livestock, again by means of sorcery. Some versions tell of the women riding on the back of a pig; this is depicted by a tapestry sewn by the local WI and hanging in the village hall.

Chapter 8

Hackleton–Horton

HACKLETON

This place name is recorded in 1086 as Hachelintone, in 1155 as Haclintona, in 1202 as Hakelinton, and in 1200 as Hakelington. Here is an Old English or Saxon name with its origins in *ing tun* following a personal name, telling us it was once 'the farmstead of the family or followers of Haeccel'.

At the White Hart, locals can enjoy a drink, although whether this is the generic name for the pub or an earlier heraldic image referring to Richard II is unclear.

HANNINGTON

Early forms of this name include Hanintone in 1086 and Haninton in 1195, which comes from a Saxon personal name with the Old English *ing tun*. This place began life as 'the farmstead of the family or followers of Hana'.

HARDINGSTONE

From 1086 comes the record of Hardingestorp, in the twelfth century it was Hardingesthorn, which, by 1224, had become Hardingstone. Compare the latter two records and one can see how the true origin has become confused and has brought about the modern suffix of -ton or -stone. This name comes from an Old English personal name with the element *thorn* and giving 'Hearding's thorn (tree)'.

Both Cotton End and Far Cotton, names for different places, are derived from the 'distant cottages'. Delapre Abbey is only known as such for, while the earliest records are in Latin, this becomes de la Preez in 1316, a name from Old French *de la pred* meaning 'of the meadows'.

The Crown Inn shows an allegiance to both monarchy and the nation.

HARDWICK

Here we have a place name found throughout the land, sometimes as Hardwicke but always with the same origins. Here we find the Old English *heorde wic* or 'specialised farm for the herd or livestock'. Old records of this name are found as Heordewican in 1067, Herdewiche in 1086, and Herdewic in 1164.

Road sign at Hannington.

Tollemache Arms, Hannington.

Merrydale Lodge was constructed in the area already known as *myrig dael* or 'the pleasant valley'.

HARGRAVE

This place name has early listings of Haregrave in 1086 and Haregraue in 1220. This could be taken from one of several combinations of two Old English elements. The first word could be *hara* meaning 'hare' or *har*, which could be used as either 'boundary' or even 'military'. It is followed by an element which could be *graf* or *greafe*, which is almost certainly 'grove' but could be seen to be 'grey'. Altogether, this could be 'grove where hares are seen', 'hoar grove', 'boundary grove', 'grove of the army', or possibly 'grey grove'.

In times when many wayside inns offered the chance to hire a small horse or pony, it clearly paid to advertise, and names such as the Old Nags Head were common. The addition of 'Old' here probably means 'former', as in referring to this being the site of the old pub known as such.

HARLESTONE

Records of this name are found as Herolvestune in 1086 and Herleston in 1170, both pointing to the Old English origin of 'the farmstead of a man called either Heoruwulf or Herewulf'. The suffix here is the most common in England's place names, *tun*, which could have a variety of meanings. However, all are basically saying it is a farming community and this book will continue to refer to where the farmers themselves lived by describing it as a 'farmstead'.

Dudman's Plantation comes from a personal name, that of Dudeman. Fleet Farm would normally be seen as coming from Old English *fleot* or 'tidal creek', yet clearly that cannot be the case here. Perhaps this is from *fliten* and thus 'the land in dispute', yet without records of such, it is difficult to be certain.

HARPER'S BROOK

The earliest surviving record is from 1270 as Harperesbrok. This is undoubtedly from Old English *hearpere* and refers to 'the brook of the harper', although it is also likely that this is used as a personal name here.

HARPOLE

This name comes from the Old English or Saxon *horu pol* or '(the place at) the muddy or dirty pool'. It is listed in Domesday as Horpol and in 1202 as Horepol.

Flitnell Barn probably features the same element seen in a minor name in Harlestone. Here is Old English *fliten hyll*, which describes 'the disputed hill'.

The Turnpike public house shows us the site of a toll house, the name referring to the spiked barrier which was first erected purely for defensive purposes. Also here is the Live and Let Live, a name where the landlord is making a comment on some dispute and normally one which he considers unjustifiable.

HARRINGTON

A name found in 1086 as Arintone, in 1148 as Hederingeton, in 1228 as Hetheringtone, and in 1249 as Hetherington. Here a Saxon personal name is followed by the Old English elements *ing* and *tun*, which gives us 'the estate of the man called Heathuhere'.

Local names include Loatland Wood, a combination of Old Swedish *lot* and Old Scandinavian *lundr* telling us it was 'the sheep pasture by the wood'. Wharf Lodge may seem obvious, but this was not used in the modern sense for some time. Here the name comes from Old Norse *vartha* or 'cairn, heap of stones', a name still seen in local fields which show pronunciation as wharf and warth and everything in between.

The Tollemache family inherited the estate somewhere around 1670, following the marriage of Sir Lionel Tollemache to Elizabeth Stanhope, and it stayed in the family until sold in 1864. Originally called the Red Cow, the local pub was renamed the Tollemache Arms to commemorate long-serving rector the Honourable Hugh Tollemache.

This church contains a speaking trumpet, one of eight known in the country. Claimed to be the invention of Sir Samuel Morland in his book of 1672, this seventeenth-century academic was also an accomplished diplomat, an inventor, noted mathematician and a spy who is held to have made significant developments in early steam power, hydraulics and even computing.

HARRINGWORTH

Records of this name include Haringeworde in 1086, Haringewurtha in 1167, and Haringworthe in 1226. This name originates in the Old English language spoken from Saxon times. This speaks of 'the dwellers of the enclosure at the stony place' and comes from the elements *haer inga worth*.

Turtle Bridge is a corruption of the name of Ralph Turcle, here by 1247, although this is a Scandinavian surname.

The local is the White Swan, a name which is probably heraldic and representative of the Vintners' Company.

HARTWELL

Just two listings of note for this name, as Hertewelle in 1086 and as Hertwella in 1155. Here we have two elements from the Old English language, *heorot* and *wella*, telling us this was '(the place at) the spring or stream where harts or stags were frequently seen'.

Bozenham Mill stood on what was previously 'Bosa's spur of land', while Laythick Copse is from *leah thiccan* or 'the thicket of or by the woodland clearing'.

The Rose & Crown shows loyalty to both England and the monarchy; it has even reached the ears of the Disney Corporation for the theme park in that corner of Florida has a pub of the name.

HASELBECH

The first element here could probably be guessed, it coming from Old English *haesel* and referring to the tree. This is followed by *bece*, a word from the same language and referring to a water course in a natural hollow. Recorded as Esbece in 1086, in the pages of Domesday, and later exactly as in the modern form as early as 1202.

HELLIDON

The great work that is Domesday recorded this name as Eliden in 1086, with later listings as Helidon in 1193, and as Haliden in 1246. This name seems to come from the Old English *haelig denu*, meaning the '(place at) the holy, healthy, or prosperous valley'. The confusion over the exact meaning of the first element is due to it being used in several places to describe each of the examples, yet never with this suffix, so it is difficult to know what was being said.

Within this parish, we find Attlefield Barn, the name referring to the settlement which was once referred to as 'Aetla's open land'. Leam Pool is of little significance here, but the springs which bubble up here feed the River Leam, which marks the boundary with neighbouring Warwickshire, then flows on as one of the major tributaries of the Avon, thereafter joining the Severn at Tewkesbury, before flowing into the sea via the Bristol Channel.

HELMDON

Records of this name include Elmedene in 1086, Helmendene in 1112, Halmeden in 1163, and Helmedene in 1249. Here is a Saxon personal name followed by Old English *denu* giving 'Helma's valley'.

Fatland Barn is a descriptive name, telling us this was 'bounteous, highly productive cultivated land', and a name which is usually applied to good pasture producing excellent dairy produce rather than referring to crops.

Locals enjoy a drink at the Bell Inn, for years one of the two places in the village where the community met, the other being the church, and the pub name links them.

HELPSTON

When listed as Hylpestun in 948, and as Helpeston in 1163, this place was a part of Northamptonshire and hence its inclusion. Oddly enough, the name still represents 'Help's *tun* or farmstead' just that single letter having changed in over a thousand years.

Local names include Rice Wood from Old English *hris* or 'brushwood'.

This was the birthplace of John Clare, who earned the sobriquet of the 'Northamptonshire peasant poet', as he only began to write in a successful attempt to stave off the eviction of his parents from their cottage. Following his death in 1864 at the age of seventy, his work has been re-evaluated and he is now considered one of the most important poets of the nineteenth century.

HEMINGTON

Listings of this name are found as Hemingtune, Hemintone, and Heminctona in 1077, 1086 and 1149 repectively. From a Saxon personal name followed by the Old English *ing tun*, this was 'Hemma or Hemmi's estate'.

HIGHAM FERRERS

From the Old English *heah ham*, this is 'the high (literally chief) homestead'. Being a fairly common name, it has acquired an addition in the name of the Ferrers family, who were her from at least the twelfth century. Records of the name have been found as Hehham in 1066, Hecham in 1086, and Heccham Ferrar in 1279.

Here we find Duchy Farm, a reminder that this manor was a part of the large amount of land held by the Duchy of Lancaster.

Henry Chichele is one of Higham Ferrers' most famous residents. Born here in 1363, he was to become Archbishop of Canterbury (1414-43).

Pub names here include the Green Dragon, a heraldic image representing the earls of Pembroke, the Old Swan, suggesting there was a former building known as the Swan, and the Griffin is the fabulous creature supposedly derived from eagle and lion, the greatest of birds and king of the beasts, and thus adopted by many families as their crest.

HINTON

A very common name which has two distinct sources. Here, the origins are Old English *hiwan tun* or 'the farmstead of the religious community'. Listings of this name include Hintone in 1086, Hinton in 1112, and Hyneton in 1199.

HINTON-IN-THE-HEDGES

As with the previous name, this is 'the farmstead of the religious community'. Recorded as Hintone in 1086, Hinton in 1202, and Hynton in 1254, the addition is not seen before the fifteenth century but was likely in use well before this, for it comes from Old English *hecg* meaning exactly what it seems: 'among the hedges'.

Steane Park was the estate of Thomas Crewe, the family giving their name to the Crewe Arms. The pub has a particularly long cellar, said by some to be the remains of a tunnel which linked the main house, pub and church.

HOLCOT

The only other record of note is that of Holcote, found consistently from 1086 until the modern form became the accepted one. This name features two words of Old English origin, *hol cot*, which tell us this was 'the cottage(s) in the hollow(s)'.

HOLDENBY

This place has been found as Aldenesbi in 1086 and as Haldenebi in 1170. Here is an Old Scandinavian personal name followed with *by* and telling us it was 'Halfdan's village'.

The name of Twigden Spinney is nothing to do with those small branches which are so readily broken off; this name comes from the family of George Twigden, who were certainly here by 1650.

HOLLOWELL

Domesday records this name as Holewelle in 1086. Undoubtedly, this comes from the Old English *hol weg* or 'the road in a hollow'.

HORTON

Recorded as Hortone in 1086, it occurs in the modern form as early as 1220. This a fairly common place name, found throughout the country and always from Old English *horu tun* or 'the dirty or muddy farmstead'.

Cheyney Farm was home to Ralph de Cheney by 1220.

Chapter 9

Irchester–Isham

IRCHESTER

This name is found as early as 973 as Yranceaster, with later listings of Irencestre in 1086, and Irecestr in 1168. Here is an Old English name, with a personal name followed by the element *caester* giving us 'Yra or Ira's Roman stronghold'.

For a long time, it was thought that the names ending in -chester or -cester were Latin names from *castra*. However, it was eventually realised that it made more sense to give the Saxon *caester*, for if there is an Old English word used to describe a Roman stronghold, it must have been used. Furthermore, the Romans themselves would have referred to it simply as a fortification, thus it makes no sense to give anything but the Saxon origin. Although note both *caester* and *castra* have similar meaning, spelling and pronunciation and doubtless have a common ancestry in the Indo-European language group.

Local names include Knuston, which is certainly 'Cnut's farmstead' but should not be considered to be the king for it was a fairly common personal name. Wymington Spinney is found on the county boundary, taking its name from Wymington in neighbouring Bedfordshire.

Local pubs include the Carpenters Arms, a common sign showing how many innkeepers of yesteryear performed more than one service to the community. The other pub is the 19th Hole, the traditional name given to the club house at a golf course.

IRTHLINGBOROUGH

Few places in Northamptonshire have records dating from earlier than this. This does not suggest that Irthlingborough is particularly older, just that records have been better maintained. Such listings include Yrtlinga burg in 780, Erdinburne in 1086, Hyrtlingberi in 1137, Urtlingburch in 1179, Hertlingburc in 1199, and Ertlingeburc in 1203. Here is a name taken from the Old English *erthling* or *yrthling burh*, which can be understood as 'the fortified manor of the ploughmen'.

The Horseshoe is a pub name which started out as a simple sign of good luck; however, the shoe must be hung with the two ends pointing upwards to prevent the luck running out. Such a sign was once considered to offer certain protection against witches.

ISE, RIVER

A tributary of the Nene, which is found as Ysan in 963 and as Yse in 1270. This name has the same origins as the Ouse, a British (or earlier) river name meaning quite simply 'water'.

ISHAM

A name seen as Ysham and Isham since the late tenth century and undoubtedly known as such well before. Here we have an Old English suffix, *hamm,* with a river name from the much earlier Celtic tongue. Thus this is '(the place at) the water meadow alongside the River Ise'. Although it may seem overly simplistic, the river name really does come from the term 'water', as do so many others from this era.

Local pubs include the Lilacs Inn, named after the flower which adorns the tree in late spring and the sign all year long. The Monk & Minstrel answers two requirements of a pub name, alliteration and linking two unlikely elements – it also suggests the place is suitable for those from all walks of life.

Chapter 10

Kelmarsh–Kislingbury

KELMARSH

No shortage of early records for this place. From the end of the eleventh to the beginning of the thirteenth centuries, we find listings of Keilmerse, Cailmarc, Keilmers, and Chailesmers. These all point to an origin of '(the place at) the marsh marked out by poles' and then from the Old English *cegel mersc*. That the name begins with a 'k' is due to the Scandinavian influence in the area.

KETTERING

One of the major towns in the county has a name which speaks of 'the settlement of the family or followers of Cytra'. This Old English place name has a Saxon personal name followed by *ingas*, listed as aet Cytringan in 956, Keteiringan in 963, Kyteringas in 972, Cateringe in 1086, and Ketering in 1200.

Bellfoundry Lane was the site of Thomas Eayre's foundry. The man was most versatile, turning his hand to clock making and a more than competent painter of landscapes. However, it is his foundry for which he is best remembered; his bells still hang in churches at Brixworth, Long Buckby, Daventry, Old, and Rothwell.

Locally, we also find the names of Links Lodge, from *hlince* or 'ridge of land', and Wadcroft, which describes 'the croft where woad was grown', and thus we cannot only see the small holding where this plant grows but also know the Saxons were growing it to dye cloth blue.

Kettering was the birthplace of artist Sir Alfred East (1844-1913), and was where Charles Wicksteed settled in 1877 and later founded Wicksteed Park, the first theme park on mainland Britain. His name is immortalised in the naming of the art gallery and of East Street. Another artist and acquaintance of East was Thomas Cooper Gotch, whose brother, John Alfred Gotch, was a renowned architect, and both are commemorated by Gotch Close and Gotch Road.

Few places in Northamptonshire have such a diverse selection of street names as those found in Kettering. A theme of trees is seen in Chestnut Avenue, Hazel Road, Larch Road, Linden Avenue, Pine Road, Lilac Place, Ash Road, Elm Road, Oak Road, Beech Crescent, Fir Road, and Poplar Road.

The royal family are seen in the names of Victoria Street, Albert Street, Alexandra Street, King Street, Princes Street and Regent Street. Former political figures are marked by Gladstone Street, after former prime minister William Ewart Gladstone, and Rosebery Street, which recalls another prime minister in Lord Rosebery. Those from the literary

Entrance to Kelmarsh Hall.

Kettering welcomes us.

world include Masefield Road (after John Masefield), Shelley Road (recalls Percy Bysshe Shelley), Wordsworth Road (after poet William Wordsworth), Burns Road (from Robert Burns), Shakespeare Road (after the Bard himself), Keats Drive (remembers poet John Keats), Eliot Close (a reminder of George Eliot, the pseudonym of novelist Mary Evans), and Kingsley Avenue (after novelist Henry Kingsley, brother of Charles).

Tordoff Place is named after the local engineering company. Burghley Street, Balfour Street and Exeter Street are named after Lord Bughley, sixteenth-century Sheriff of Northamptonshire whose family were also earls of Exeter. Shaftesbury Street is named after the earls of Shaftesbury; the family were also earls of Devonshire and Northampton. Granville Street recalls Granville Leveson-Gower, 1st Earl Granville, who was born in Northamptonshire. With a residence in the county, the many titles of the Duke of Buccleuch are seen in Buccleuch Street and Eskdaill Street, and the Earl of Dalkeith public house, while Montagu Street takes the family name. There is also a public house called the Buccleuch. Spencer Street is named after the earls Spencer, based in Northamptonshire. Sydney Street remembers Thomas Townshend, 1st Viscount Sydney.

The Treshams were landlords by the seventeenth century, hence the naming of Tresham Lane. William Carey spent his life in the town before departing for India in 1793 as a missionary. A colleague of Carey's, Andrew Fuller, is remembered by Fuller Street. William Knibb was born in Market Street, he was also a missionary and yet it was probably efforts in the emancipation of slaves which led to the naming of Knibb Street. Toller Place is another marking the efforts of a religious family, here the father and son preached in the town for a combined total of exactly one hundred years.

What was once Workhouse Lane was renamed Dryland Street in the very early twentieth century to honour the recently departed John Winter Dryland. It was here, on the corner with High Street, that Dr Dryland set up his practice in 1857. He took a great deal of interest in the workhouse and was most influential there, as he was at the local post office, railway authority, and the fire brigade. His son, Leslie Dryland, took over his father's surgery, which was open until 1941.

Pubs in Kettering include the Melton Arms, which takes the name of the street where it stands, with Melton Street itself transferred from the Leicestershire town. The nation's wealth was once founded upon sheep, or more correctly, wool. Hence the name of the Woolpack Inn, which refers to the standard bale of 240 pounds in weight, while the Woolcomber is a pub name reminding us of how the tangled wool once had to be combed out laboriously by hand. Another fabric is seen in the name of the Leather Craftsman, probably a sideline or earlier career of a landlord, as was the case with the Bakers Arms, and also the Cordwainer.

Reminders of days when the pub was the service station of its age are common; in Kettering, we find the Wayfarers, who could well have been heading for the Old Market Inn. Trees were common signposts to pubs and the Cherry Tree Inn is a local example. These are often seen in former open country, as are names such as the Shire Horse, the Briars, and also the Warren.

Birds are popular as they are visually appealing and easily recognised, as is the case with the Swan Hotel and the Peacock Inn. However, the Beeswing is nothing to do with the insect, but is a term used to describe the film which forms on port and other fortified wines when they have been kept for many years and thus is an advertisement for fine wine. The same is true of the Sportsmans Arms, suggesting this is the meeting place for those who follow sporting pursuits, also seen in the Talbot Hotel which is named after the hunting dog.

The Samuel Pepys Inn is one of only four in the country, named after the man (1633-1703) whose diaries made him a household name, although they were written in code and not published until 1825, providing an insight into the Restoration period and including the Plague and the Great Fire of London. However, these records only covered the years 1660-69 inclusive; the rest of the time he was rather busy working as a naval official and also served a term as President of the Royal Society.

KILSBY

From Kildesbig in 1043, Kyldesby in 1050, and Kildebi in 1139, through to Kildesbi in 1155, this can be seen to be a hybrid of an Old English prefix followed by the common Old Scandinavian element *by* meaning 'village'. The first element is undoubtedly *cild*; however, although this is a well-known element, it is difficult to understand the use here. This element is today seen as 'child' but had a different meaning when the place was first settled as 'the young nobleman'. However, the same spelling was also a personal name; thus the name must be defined as 'the village of the young nobleman or a man called Cild'. The initial 'k' instead of 'c' is a result of the Scandinavian influence. It is highly unlikely that any proof of which origin will ever be discovered.

The name of Arnills Gate is a corruption of the name of the Arnold family who were living here, George Arnold the earliest named who was here by the eighteenth century.

KING'S CLIFFE

The basic name here is the second part. It is derived from the Old English *clif* and means '(the place at) the cliff'. It is a fairly common place name and thus there is the addition which tells us it was a royal manor; indeed, it was named as such in Domesday. Listings of this name have been found as Clive in 1086 and Cliua in 1100.

Buxton Wood is named after Roger Bucstan, who was here by 1247; Calvey Wood comes from *calu* meaning 'bare' and showing the soil was not particularly rich; and Law's Lawn is named after William Lawe, who was here in 1605, and who was an ancestor of William Law (1686-1761), the cleric and writer who penned *A Serious Call to a Devout and Holy Life* who was born in King's Cliffe.

One man who took the link with the King to extraordinary lengths was Michael Hudson, a rector of King's Cliffe. In the seventeenth century, at the outbreak of the English Civil War, Hudson was a royal chaplain; however, unknown to most, he was also serving the King by acting as a courier. In the year of 1646 alone, he was captured no less than three times by Cromwell's forces, who released him once; the other times he escaped – the second time screening his face with a basket of apples on his head.

Two years later and he was returning with new recruits from East Anglia when they were met by Parliamentarian forces at Woodcroft Castle in neighbouring Lincolnshire. Outnumbered, Hudson and his men were driven back; he eventually found himself trapped on the battlements, from which he was flung over the edge into the moat below. Half drowned, he was pulled out and clubbed about the head with the butt of a musket until dead. His tongue was then cut out and paraded as a trophy.

KING'S SUTTON

With records of Sudtone in 1086 and Suttun Regis in 1252, there are no prizes for seeing the similarity with the previous name. Indeed, Domesday lists the place as being held by William the Conqueror at the time of the great survey. Sutton is one of the most common place names in the country, justifiably requiring an addition for distinction. It comes from the Old English *suth tun* meaning 'the farmstead to the south', which also tells us it was known as such by a settlement north of here, although we can never be certain which.

The name of Great Purston is derived from 'the farm of the priests', and Twyford Farm is 'the twin or double ford'.

Olga Kevelos was a resident of the village for many years, until her peaceful passing in late 2009. Born in Birmingham, she worked at the Royal Observatory in Greenwich until 1943, when she volunteered to work the narrowboats of the inland waterways during the Second World War delivering goods. Following the war, she became the only woman to win two gold medals in the International Six Days Enduro, a competition for motorcyclists; she also competed in scrambling and track racing. During the Swinging Sixties, she took over as landlady of the Three Tuns in the village, and was seen on national television competing on BBC Television's *Mastermind*. In the future, perhaps those who make such decisions will consider Olga Kevelos the ideal subject for a street name.

KINGSTHORPE

Domesday lists this name as just *Torp*; the earliest record of the modern kind is from 1190 as *Kingestorp*. This name is from the Old English *cyning* and the Old Scandinavian *thorp*; such hybrids are not unusual in the counties which fell on or near the border between Saxon England and the region dominated by the Scandinavians to the north and east. The two elements blend together well – otherwise we would expect to find two distinct words as with the previous names. Here is a place name meaning 'the outlying farmstead belonging to the crown'.

The monarchy was also in mind when two pubs were named. King William IV, who reigned from 1830 until his death seven years later, was the last king of the House of Hanover. His reign was short and uneventful; however, it did see major reforms, including those to the poor laws, child labour, and the abolition of slavery. Because he saw service in the navy, albeit with little hostility, he became known as the Sailor King. His consort provided the inspiration when naming the Queen Adelaide public house; the German-born royal also gave her name to the Australian city. The Windmill takes the name of that building, once a common sight in this country, with the Sunnyside Inn suggesting this was the nicer part in an effort to entice customers, although it has been a pilgrimage for fans of Billy Fury for many years, for this was where he played his last official engagement before his premature death in 1983 at the age of forty-two.

Streets of Kingsthorpe are named after former presidents of the United States of America. Washington Street remembers George Washington, in office 1789-97, whose ancestors came from nearby Sulgrave; Lincoln Street is named after the sixteenth president, who served 1861-65 and who was the first of that office to be assassinated;

while Garfield Street and Garfield Close remember another assasinated president, James A. Garfield, who was only in office for six months after his inauguration on 4 March 1881. His tenure of 199 days is the second shortest in history: William Harrison's lasted just thirty-two days, and would have been even shorter had he not lived another seventy-nine days after being shot in July.

KISLINGBURY

As with Kilsby, there is some dispute as to whether the first element here is a personal name or not. With listings such as Ceselingeberie, Cifeelingeberie, Cheselingebiri, and Kiselingeberia between 1086 and 1176, the name undoubtedly comes from the Old English *cisel inga burh*. This is quite easy to see as being 'the stronghold of the dwellers on the gravelly ground'. However, the first element may be a personal name, in which case this would be a Saxon name and speak of 'the stronghold of the family or followers of a man called Cysel'. Unless further evidence is found, it seems the name will always remain uncertain.

Bly Lane gets its name from a tributary of the River Nene, a name meaning 'blithe, peaceful' and describing its smooth flow. Interestingly, while the lane name survives, the river, undoubtedly once known as the Blythe, is now nameless on all maps.

Locals enjoy a drink in the Old Red Lion which, without the 'Old', is the most common pub name in England and is linked heraldically to the House of Stuart and John of Gaunt. Adding 'Old' to a name suggests great age, yet there is rarely any truth in an early date for such places. Thus perhaps it would be better to see these names as 'older', although a suggestion of great age may also be used to suggest 'traditional'. Whilst it may never have been the basis for any pub name, the number of Red Lion pubs led to the throat being termed 'Red Lion Lane' in some areas.

Chapter 11

Lamport–Lutton

LAMPORT

For the author, the most pleasing aspect in defining place names is when they produce an amazingly clear and instantaneous image of the site as it was when first named. Here we have an example of such.

This name is found as Langeport in Domesday and later. Despite what has been said about the unreliability of the great survey's record of proper names, and a selection of early forms are required for the most accurate definitions, this single record is enough to tell us the origins of this name. From the Old English *lang port* comes the 'place of the long market place'.

Firstly, this tells us the place was quite obviously extended, rather than the usual roughly circular habitation around a central point, while we also see the place was a centre for trade. Furthermore, it is possible to state this market would have existed for a substantial length of time in order for the name to become fixed. Knowing what the people wore, what foods they ate, and having a good idea of their lifestyle, we just need a moment to assemble these thoughts to form a picture of life in Lamport during the Saxon period.

The name of Blueberry Lodge has no connection with fruit; it comes from Old English *blaw beorg* and describes 'the cold or exposed hill'.

LAXTON

This name is also found further north in Nottinghamshire and Yorkshire where the name was a Lax-ing-ton, but has become abbreviated. In Northamptonshire, it is found as *Lastone*, which tells of 'Leaxa's farmstead' and with the personal name being followed by the common Old English *tun*.

Both Spanhoe Farm and Spanhoe Wood share a common origin in 'chips of wood from the projecting land'. However, it is not clear if this comes from Old English *span hoh* or if the first element here is Old Norse *spann*, although the meaning is the same in either case.

LILBOURNE

A place name recorded as Lilleburne and Lilleburna in the eleventh century. We can be quite certain this comes from a Saxon personal name followed by the Old English *burna* giving the meaining of 'stream of a man named Lilla'.

LITCHBOROUGH

In 1086, Domesday records the place as Liceberge, in 1199, Lichebarue, and three years later as Licheberw. Here is an Old English place name from *lycce beorg* telling us of the '(place at) the hill with an enclosure'.

The name of Redmore Farm is derived from Old English *read hreod* and describes 'the reedy or red moorland'.

LITTLE ADDINGTON

There are several places with this name in the country, all with the same meaning. Recorded as Edintone in 1086, Edintona in 1130, and as Maior Adinton in 1220, here is a Saxon personal name followed by the Old English *ing tun*, giving us 'the estate associated with a man called Eadda or Aeddi'.

A former rector here is said to have had an affair with a girl from Denford during the fifteenth century. When she disappeared, she was thought to have been murdered and buried at Vicarage Farm. When this area was developed in the twentieth century, it was claimed the girl's spirit had been awakened.

LITTLE BILLING

Domesday's record in 1086 is as Belinge, with a later record of Billingge Magna in the thirteenth century. Here is another Saxon personal name followed by an Old English suffix *ingas*, which shows us this was the '(settlement) of the family or followers of a man called Bill or Billa'.

LITTLE BRINGTON

No prizes for seeing this is the smaller of the two settlements with this name. The smaller version is listed as Brinintone, Brintone, Brinton, and Little Bryton from the eleventh to the thirteenth centuries, all of which point to this being 'the farmestead associated with the family or followers of a man called Bryni'.

LITTLE HARROWDEN

This name has listings such as Hargedone in 1086, Harewedon in 1202, and Parva Harewedon in 1220. Clearly there is a larger settlement of the same name, this being less than half a mile away. Both originate in Old English *hearg-dun*, which describes this as '(the place at) the hill of the heathen shrines or temples'. Just which god or gods were worshipped here is unknown and will probably remain so.

A reminder of a major employer at Long Buckby.

LITTLE HOUGHTON

Once again, this is the smaller of two similarly named places in Northamptonshire. Recorded as Hoctune in 1086 and as Magna Houtona in 1199, this name has more than a dozen examples around the country. With a couple of exceptions, they are all derived from the Old English *hoh-tun*: 'the farmstead of or by the ridge or hill spur'.

LODDINGTON

Early records of this name are plentiful, ranging from Ludintone in 1086, through Ludinton in 1125, Ludington in 1248, to Lodington in 1209. Here we have a Saxon personal name followed by Old English *ing tun*, giving 'the estate associated with a man called Loda or Lod'.

LONG BUCKBY

Recorded as Buchebi in 1086 and as Longe Bugby in 1565, this is of Scandinavian origins and describes 'the village of a man called Bukki or Bucca'. Clearly the addition refers to the length of the village, which is aligned along its main road, to differentiate from Lower Buckby.

The Peacock at Long Buckby.   The Admiral Rodney at Long Buckby.

There is also a Long Buckby Wharf, clearly a reference to the Grand Union Canal which passes through here and shows this particular part of the place did not exist until the coming of the canals. Three Bridges Road leads into these settlements from the north – a name which also could not have existed before the eighteenth-century canal (the only route it passes over), nor indeed the nineteenth-century railway, or even the M1 motorway, which opened on 2 November 1959.

Cotton End is located 'at the cottages'; Hoborough Hill really does not need the additional part of the name for the basic name already describes 'the hollow hill'; Surney Bridge and Surney Lodge are located 'south of the *eg* or well-watered land'; Greenhill Farm was associated with Simon de Grenehille by 1330; and Leighton lodge took its name from Old English *leac tun* describing 'a vegetable garden'.

Pubs here include the Admiral Rodney, named after Admiral George Brydges Rodney, 1st Baron Rodney (1719-92), a naval officer whose career was steady without being exceptional. On land, he became the parliamentary representative for Saltash in 1751 before marrying Jane Compton, the sister of Charles Compton, 7th Earl of Northampton. In 1768, he successfully fought to represent Northampton, although the cost almost proved his financial undoing. The Peacock is not always used as a heraldic image; the sheen of its plumage and the magnificent tail make it instantly recognisable.

Other roads here represent its history. The hamlet of Murcott, a name meaning 'the cottages at the marsh', gave a name to Murcott Close. Tebbitts Close remembers the landowners and farmers who included George Edward Tebbitt, who was here in the nineteenth century. Shopkeeper Reuben Philips was a nineteenth-century representative of the family who gave their name to Philips Way. Kingston Close and

Marriotts Road take their names from the Kingstons and the Marriotts, longtime local farming families. Church Street is named after the local church of St Lawrence, while Skinyard Lane is a reminder of where animal skins were cured for many years.

The marriage of Lady Diana Spencer to the Prince of Wales saw her become a member of the House of Windsor, as are their two sons Prince William and Prince Harry. All are commemorated in the naming of Spencer Road, Harry's Close, Windsor Close, William Road, and Charles Close.

LOWER BUCKBY

The only records for this name are as Buchebi and Buckeby in 1086 and 1203 respectively. Almost certainly this comes from the Old Scandinavian suffix *by* preceded by a personal name and giving "Bukki's village'. However, there is a small possibility the personal name is that of a Saxon, in which case it would be 'Bucca's village'.

LOWER BENEFIELD

In 970, this place is recorded as Beringafeld and in Domesday as Benefeld. Here is a Saxon personal name followed by the Old English *inga feld*, which tells us of the '(place at) the open land of the family or followers of a man called Bera'.

LOWICK

Recorded as Luhwic, Lofwyc, and Luffewich in the eleventh and twelfth centuries, this is a name of Saxon origins. Here the personal name is followed by the common Old English element *wic*, which allows us to define this name as 'Luhha or Luffa's specialised farm'. Almost always, these farms specialised in dairy produce; however, without further evidence, it is impossible to be completely certain.

From Old English *bula oetsce*, the locally named Bullicks Wood describes 'the pasture for rearing bulls'. Drayton House is a common minor place name; from Old English *draeg tun*, this is 'the portage' and where goods were dragged for any of numerous reasons.

The image of the fox has long been a favourite on the sign outside pubs. However, it is so common that many have sought to expand upon the basic name and, as here with the Snooty Fox, develop the image of the fox as the stereotypical dandy.

LUTTON

This name is listed as Lundingtun in 972, Ludintune in 1060, and Luditone in 1086, which shows the modern form to be an abbreviation. Here, the Old English origin is 'the estate associated with a man called Luda', from the Saxon personal name followed by *ing tun*.

Chapter 12

Maidford–Moulton

MAIDFORD

Here we have a name which has as obvious an origin today as it did when it was first coined. Listed in Domesday as Merdeford, in 1167 as Maideneford, and in 1200 as Meideford, this is undoubtedly from Old English *maegden ford* or 'the ford of the maidens'.

However, the question here is not what but why this origin. Clearly the name had some significance, yet the appearance of a group of women at a stream is hardly unusual. It has been suggested the maidens were nuns; however, this does not seem plausible, for the reference would surely have been specifically to the religious order. Thoughts of ancient pagan fertility ceremonies must also be discounted. There is no reason to believe Christianity took hold here very much later than elsewhere; if so, there would be other evidence to support this.

Whatever the reason for the maidens meeting here, it must have been not only reasonably unique but also continued for a significant period of time. There has been speculation of an alternative origin, *maegth*, speaking of the plant 'mayweed', but this has had little support. Why the women met here seems destined to remain a mystery, which makes it even more intriguing.

The name of Burntfold Copse takes its name from the 'area cleared by burning near the copse where animals were held'.

MAIDWELL

As with the previous entry, the naming of this place is something of an enigma. Records have been found of Medewelle in 1086 and Maidewell in 1198, both point to the same Old English first element as the previous name here suffixed by *wella* and giving us 'the spring or stream of the maidens'.

As with the previous name, there is no known reason why the women would be associated with the place or the stream, yet that they were here regularly and for some significant period of time is unquestionable.

Berrydale Covert gets its name from *burh dael*, which refers to 'the valley with or by a fortification'. Scotland Wood has no connection with north of the border, here *scot land* refers to 'the land with a tax or other payment'.

MARSTON ST LAWRENCE

There are over twenty reasonably sized places in the country called Marston, hence the additions for distinction. All come from Old English *mersc tun*, giving 'farmstead of or by the marshland'. Domesday lists the name as Merestone, while the earliest record with the addition is as Mersshton Sancti Laurencii in 1329, which is quite obviously the dedication of the local church.

From a description meaning 'the place of cottages' comes a name which was later applied to a more modern building known as Costow House.

MARSTON TRUSSELL

As with the previous name, this is 'the farmstead on or near the marsh' from Old English *mersc tun*. The addition here is manorial, a reminder that the place was held by the Trussel family, who were here by the thirteenth century, while the name is recorded as Mersitone in 1086 and Merston Trussel in 1236.

MAXEY

Another place which is no longer in Northamptonshire; however, until county boundaries were changed in 1974, they had largely stood unaltered since the Saxons used these divisions over one thousand years ago. Found in 963 as Macusie and as Makeseia in 1199, this name shows how these wetlands had dry areas which were settled and referred to as islands. Here the name is 'Maccus's *eg* or island'.

Locally, the names of Lolham Hall, Lolham Bridge and Lolham Mill all share a name which has its origins in Old English *hleo helm* or 'the cattle shed on a projection of land'.

MEARS ASHBY

Within the region where the Scandinavian influence was greatest in England, to the north and east, this must be one of the most common names. There are two potential origins, most often Old Scandinavian *askr–by*, 'the village where the ash trees grow'. However, sometimes the first element is Old English *aesc*, but the meaning is exactly the same.

Most of these common place names have a second additional element which gives a unique quality to the name. Here it is the de Mares family, who were lords of this manor from the thirteenth century. The place is recorded as Asbi in 1086 and by 1282 is seen as Esseby Mares.

MIDDLETON

Listed as Middelton in 1197, this is a common name and, as with the following name, describes 'the middle farmstead'.

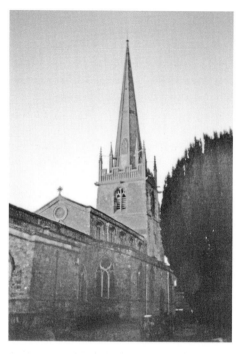

All Saints church at Middleton Cheney in the morning light.

Swinawe Wood is from *swine haga*, 'the enclosure for pigs', and Yokewood Lodge tells us someone specialised in making 'wooden yokes'.

MIDDLETON CHENEY

Another common basic name with a distinctive second element. The name is recorded as Mideltone in 1086 and as Middleton Cheyndut in 1342. This comes from the Old English *middel tun* meaning 'the middle farmstead' and between two other farmsteads. Here, the addition is manorial, telling us of the de Chendut family who were from at least the twelfth century.

The Holt has not changed at all since Saxon times when *holt* meant exactly what it does today, a 'small wood, thicket'. Overthorpe features the element *thorp* or 'outlying farmstead' here in a more elevated position.

MILTON MALSOR

There are similarites between this and the previous name. Records show this as being recorded as Mideltone in 1086 and Milton alias Middleton Malsor as late as 1781. Clearly the name had exactly the same origins as Middleton Cheney; from the Old English *middel tun*, this is 'the middle farmstead', just this has become somewhat slurred and, as shown by the late entry from the eighteenth century, is a comparatively late contraction. The addition is manorial, although the Malsor family were here many years before the records show their name was part of the place; indeed, there is evidence of this name in documents from the twelfth century.

MORETON PINKNEY

Another double-barrelled name which, just like the previous examples, has a common first element and a manorial second part. Domesday records the name as simply Mortone in 1086, while there are thirteenth century listings of Geldenemortone and Guldenemorton. The family in question here are the de Pinkeny family, who were here by the thirteenth century.

Interestingly, the name of Henry de Pinkeny, who was here in 1236, can also be traced to Picquigny in Picardy, France. Another minor name, that of Canada, normally seen as a simple remoteness name, was here also chosen to commemorate an individual born in the village, Dr Ashton Oxenden (1808-92), who was the Bishop of Montreal (1869-78).

MOULTON

A name found half a dozen times around the north and east of England, always from the Old English *mul tun*, 'the farmstead where mules are kept', or the first element may be a Saxon personal name, giving 'Mula's farmstead'. The name has been recorded as Multun in 1066, Multone in 1086, Multon in 1200, Muleton in 1202, and Molentun in 1205.

Local pubs include the White Lion, here most likely a heraldic reference to Edward IV. The Cardigan Arms refers to the Montagu family, earls of Cardigan from the eighteenth century. This village also has links with John Jeye, a man whose name is better known for the disinfectant which has been marketed for over a century as *Jeyes Fluid*.

Chapter 13

Naseby–Norton

NASEBY

Records of this place name go back to Domesday when it appears as Navesberie; by 1094, it is Navzeberia, and in 1167, Nauesbi. As noted elsewhere in the book, Northamptonshire stands along the line between the Saxon- and Scandinavian-controlled England and shows influence from both cultures. This explains why this name originally had an Old English suffix in *burh* following the Saxon personal name, telling us it was 'the stronghold of a man called Hnaef'. From the twelfth century, the Old Scandinavian *by* is in use and it should be given as 'Hnaef's village'.

That the name has endured as Nase-by, not Nase-borough, is significant. If the single record from the twelfth century was the only evidence, we could dismiss it as the misunderstanding of the name by a Scandinavian clerk. However, that it has become the accepted form seems to show the Saxons had largely disappeared sometime during the first half of the twelfth century. Thus, by the time the name is first seen with the *by* suffix, the place had been known as Naseby by the locals for some time, probably as long as any could remember.

The name of Shuckburgh Farm has been transferred from Shuckburgh in Warwickshire, coming here with those who once held this manor. Of course, the name of Naseby is synonymous with the battle of 1645; thus it is no surprise to find the names of two of the major figures in the wars marked in Cromwell House and Prince Rupert's Farm.

A less well-known claim to fame than the battle is marked by a monument in the grounds of Manor Farm. Here is the source of the River Avon, more often referred to as the Warwickshire Avon.

NASSINGTON

Only two forms of note have been found, as Nassintone in 1086 and Nessinton in 1171. Here, the three Old English elements are undoubtedly *naess ing tun*; however, the interpretation is less certain. It has been said to be 'the farmstead on the promontory', yet this definition does not take the middle element into consideration. Thus, this name should probably be given as 'the farmstead of the people of the promontory'. This also suggests there was once more than one settlement in close proximity, most likely not contemporary but from different eras.

Local names include Old Sulehay and New Sulehay, names derived from 'Seofa's *leah* or woodland clearing'. Ring Law gets its name from 'an enclosure held by a group of drengs', from Old Norse *drengi*. A dreng was a free man, one who joined with other drengs to lord it over a small manor on payment and services to the Crown. Whether this should be considered free peasantry is still a matter for debate.

NENE, RIVER

A name found as Nyn in 948 and as Nen in 1228, here is a name of unknown etymology which is certainly from at least the Celtic era and probably even earlier.

NETHER HEYFORD

In Domesday, this place is seen as Heiforde, in 1197, it becomes Heyford, while the addition is first seen in 1220 as Inferior Heyford. This is a name which produces an instant image, a mental snapshot, of life during the Saxon era, for it describes 'the ford used mainly during hay-making time' from Old English *heg ford*. The name is found four times in England, in neighbouring Oxfordshire and here where the name differentiates from Upper Heyford.

The Foresters Arms here refers to the Ancient Order of Foresters, a well-supported friendly society with 'courts' or meeting places in both the UK and the US.

NEWBOROUGH

This name tells us it was 'the new fortification', that is, new in comparison with nearby Borough Fen, itself being 'the fortification in the wetland'.

Local names include Gray's Farm, worked by Thomas Gray's family in the seventeenth century, and Baxter's Bridge, associated with Leonard Baxter, whose family were here by 1666. Decay Farm shows there was 'duck hunting' here, nothing to do with the modern idea of attracting ducks with decoys but from a Saxon 'duck island'. Kennulph's Drain was named from the man who was Abbot of Peterborough in 1005.

NEWBOTTLE

To those who have no knowledge of place names, this may seem the strangest of names. However, the meaning of the Old English *bothl*, pronounced exactly the same as the present 'bottle', was amazingly different. Preceded by *niwe*, this name tells us it was 'the new building'; it is listed as Neubotle in 1404.

Here we find the common place name of Charlton, from Old English *ceorl tun* and describing 'the farmstead of the ceorls or peasants'.

NOBOTTLE

Three early forms for this name Nevbote in 1086, Neubottle in 1200, and Neuwebotle in 1202. As with the previous name, this comes from the Old English *niwe bothl*,

The Monkey's Head public house, Northampton.

meaning 'the new building'. Clearly in both cases, the building in question must have been of impressive or unusual construction.

NORTHAMPTON

The name of the county town was once much shorter. It is recorded as Hamtun in 917, Hamton in 972, Northhamtun in 1065 and both Hantone and Northantone. The basic name comes from the Old English *ham tun* 'the homestead of the farm', the 'north' was seemingly just added to distinguish this place from Southampton, although they have different origins.

Street names of Northampton include Abington Street, which leads to the district of that name; while Angel Street takes its name from the pub, and Swan Street is named from the Swan public house. Bridge Street leads to where it crosses the River Nene; Castle Street marks the position of old Northampton Castle; College Street is named from the house of the collegiate clergy of All Saints, founded here in the fourteenth century; the goldsmiths were located in Gold Street; Tanner Street is named after those who worked with leather; while the dealers in cloth and fabrics gave their name to Mercers Row, Woolmonger Street and the road known simply as Drapery.

Bearward Street reminds us that this was 'the bear ward', that is, where the 'keeper of performing bears' resided. Mayorhold is nothing to do with the office of local government, but is a corruption of 'mare hold' and where these horses were kept.

A road leading to one of the old town gates is remembered by the name of Derngate Street, where the first part is derived from Old English *dierne* or 'hidden, secret'. Clearly, the location of the gate would hardly have been secret, thus this is understood as being rather less literal and suggesting it was simply the least significant.

Greyfriars Street, Monks Park Street and Monks Pond Street are all named from the various cells of monks which existed around the city. Similarly, the owner and proprietor of St Andrew's Priory, Sir Francis Crane, is remembered by the names of both Crane Street and Francis Street.

Wantage Road is named after Lady Wantage, a benefactor of the city in the late nineteenth century. The local financier and chairman of the Northampton Union Bank – later the National Provincial and today the NatWest – was one Henry Billington Whitworth, who gave his name to Henry Street, Billington Street and Whitworth Road.

Sir Henry Randall was a prominent figure in horse-racing circles, his children giving their names to Percy Road and Florence Road. William Collins, who was resident at Monks Park Hall when he died in 1876, subsequently gave his name to Collins Street. Thomas Purser is remembered by Purser Street; Frederick Stimpson is marked by Stimpson Street; Perry Street is named after Pickering Phipps Perry; Turner Street is a reminder of Richard Turner; Robert Derby was the inspiration for Derby Street; Adnitt Street comes from one Frederick George Adnitt; and baker Thomas Adams is commemorated by Adams Street.

Bailiff Street ran past what was once Northampton Gaol; Vernon Street and Barry Street are named after former mayors of the city; and Bruce Street remembers H. A. Bruce, who, in the nineteenth century, served as Home Secretary. Other local councillors and also, somewhat unusually, their wives are remembered by Cecil Road, Charles Street, Edith Street, and Ethel Street.

Scarletwell Street has a rather interesting etymology, for this refers to the water from this spring or stream, which was found to be an exellent medium for dying cloth an excellent scarlet colour.

There are also a large number of roads and streets named after poets in the city. Arnold Road is after Matthew Arnold (1822-88), son of the famous Rugby School headmaster Thomas Arnold and often referred to as the Third Great Victorian Poet. Burns Street is named after Robert Burns (1759-96), also variously known as Rabbie Burns, the Bard of Ayrshire, and the Ploughman Poet. Thomas Campbell (1777-1844) was the inspiration for Campbell Street, a Scottish poet who is remembered for his sentimental poetry and also wrote lyrics to stirring songs including *Ye Mariners of England*.

Lord Byron (1788-1824) is commemorated by Byron Street, a man whose private life remains as widely discussed as his work, Lady Caroline Lamb famously saying he was 'Mad, bad, and dangerous to know'.

Chaucer Street is after Geoffrey Chaucer (1343-1400), known for his *Canterbury Tales* and generally acknowledged as the Father of English Literature. Clare Street remembers John Clare (1793-1864), who died in St Andrew's Hospital in Northampton and whose work has been seen as increasingly important in the years since his death. Cowper Street is named after William Cowper (1731-1800), who was as well known for his hymns, and whose name should be pronounced 'Cooper'.

John Dryden (1631-1700) had Dryden Street named after him, mainly because he was not only born in Northamptonshire but also lived there for several years before he gained fame. Less well known is that he was a second cousin of Jonathan Swift, author of *Gulliver's Travels*. Gray Street recalls Thomas Gray (1716-71), who went to school with Horace Walpole, literary son of British prime minister Robert Walpole.

James Hervey (1714-58) gave his name to Hervey Street, his writing being second to his career as a parish priest. Hood Street takes the name of Thomas Hood (1799-1845), who was not only an accomplished writer but also produced a series of humorous illustrations. John Milton (1608-74) was the man who gave his name to Milton Street, best known for his *Paradise Lost* and *Paradise Regained*; the political upheaval in England during his lifetime influenced his thinking.

Pubs in one of the largest towns in Europe include the Crown & Cushion, a name which answers three of the requirements for a pub name: alliteration, the marketing man's dream; the inclusion of 'and' or '&', which then connects two seemingly unrelated items; and it does no harm to show allegiance to the monarchy and thus the nation. Here the link is seen at the coronation or other ceremony, when the crown is carried on a cushion to be placed ceremoniously on the head of the monarch. Other 'royal' or 'patriotic' names include the Victoria Inn, Britannia Inn, Princess Alexandra, Duke of Edinburgh, Duke of York, Prince of Wales, Crown Inn, Royal Oak, Kings Head, Rose & Crown, Old Crown Inn, George Inn, King Billy, Patriot, and Queen Victoria Inn. Conversely, we find the Cromwell Cottage: Oliver Cromwell was Lord Protector of England (1653-58) and someone whose unsavoury reputation is probably based on the politics of the day rather than the man himself. It is unclear if this was originally an anti-royal statement.

Other notable individuals and characters are commemorated: the Charles Bradlaugh is named after political activist and a noted atheist during the nineteenth century who served as MP for the town, his predessor was Sir Pickering Phipps who also had a pub named after him; Jolly Crispin is a different look at St Crispin, who paid for his own travels as a cobbler, enabling his to spread the word and who is associated with the Battle of Agincourt, for it was fought on St Crispin's Day; the Garibaldi marks the achievements of Guiseppe Garibaldi (1807-82), the Italian soldier and patriot; Punch and Judy also originated in Italy, a traditional show for children which came to our shores in the seventeenth century; Lord Byron remembers the famous romantic poet; Pomfret Arms is probably named after John Pomfret, seventeenth-century clergyman and poet whose family will have originated from Pontefract, still referred to as Pomfret by the locals; Thomas à Becket is named after the saint and former Archbishop of Canterbury who was murdered in Canterbury Cathedral in 1170; Fitzgerald Arms remembers the family who were lords of the manor of Naseby; the family who came from nearby Fawsley gave their name to the Knightley Arms; and possibly the best-known family in the county, based at Northrop, gave their name to the Spencer Arms.

To advertise former and alternative trades of the landlord on the pub sign made sense, especially if he still had the second string to his bow, as was common at the time. Alternatively, it could refer to a nearby factory or trade. Thus we find the Shoemakers Arms, Lamplighter, Gardeners Arms, Tanners, Maltsters Arms and the Malt Shovel, Foundrymans Arms, Horseshoe, Three Horseshoes, and Bricklayers Arms.

It is also commonplace to find heraldic imagery used on a pub sign or name. Thus we find the Black Lion, referring to Queen Philippa of Hainault, the consort of Edward III; the Golden Lion represents the Percy family, dukes of Northumberland; the Spread Eagle is a heraldic reference to many countries; the White Horse is a reference to the House of Hanover; the Black Horse symbolises the goldsmiths; the Red Lion points to Scotland and the House of Stuart; the griffin has been adopted in the coat of arms of countless families, hence the name of the Griffin Inn and the Griffins Head; Ye Olde

Saracens Head shows this family fought in the Crusades; the Wheatsheaf appears in the coats of arms of the Brewers' Company; the Chequers shows a moneyer was available within; and the Compass is symbolic of many trades including masons and carpenters.

The name of the Wig & Pen shows that the law courts and barristers chambers are nearby; the Blarney Stone is named after the stone set in the wall of Blarney Castle near Cork; kissing such is said to give one the gift of the gab; the Mailcoach marks a stopping-off point on the roads for the branch of the postal service made obsolete by 1846 with the coming of the railways; the Hogs Head is the name given to the large cask for wines and beers; both the Cricketers Arms and the Bat & Wickets show these places are within sight of the county cricket ground.

The Romany takes the image of the Romany Gypsy on the sign, possibly an early landlord or maybe a local character. Naming a pub the White Elephant seems an unusual decision, for it refers to an undertaking which drains rather than improves one's financial status. The Frog & Fiddler is probably a name created to answer the requirements of a basic pub name, two unrelated items with the added bonus of alliteration. In the 1940s, Bing Crosby, Bob Hope and Dorothy Lamour starred in a series of films known as the Road Pictures, one of which gave a name to the Road to Morocco public house.

Many places have a ridge of land known as Shoulder of Mutton, which was taken by the pub later built there. Similarly, the farthest corner of the parish could be referred to as World's End, hence the pub name. The Railway Tavern could not have existed before the arrival of the railways, neither could the Brampton Halt, which occupies the former stationmaster's house. Introduced to Britain in the sixteenth century, the Artichoke Inn is a plant with a distinctive shape and thus makes an excellent pub name. The Greyhound could refer to the famous mailcoaches, although it could also be a heraldic symbol representing the dukes of Newcastle. Advertising the product was always a good idea, hence the name of the Rose & Claret.

As a footnote, it is interesting to note that, in 1830, there were an astonishing 358 public houses in the county town. Of these, no less than twenty-six were in Bridge Street alone.

NORTHAMPTONSHIRE

As with many counties, here we find the county town with the addition of Old English *scir*, which literally means 'district'. This name is first found in 1011 as Hamtunscir, while Domesday refers to Northantonescire.

NORTON

Found in Domesday as Nortone and as Norton juxta Davintre in 1242, this is a common name and simply 'the northern farmstead'.

Looking around this parish, we see Mazedale Spinney, the small woodland telling it has a name meaning 'the valley of the boundary'. Muscott is derived from *musa cote*, quite literally 'the mice's cottages' and probably a derogatory term applied to what was seen as the humblest of homes. Norborough Farm gets its name from *north beorg* and refers to 'the northern hill', while Thrupp Grounds is a common minor name speaking of 'the outlying farm'.

Chapter 14

Oakley–Overstone

OAKLEY (GREAT AND LITTLE)

With listings of Achelau in Domesday, as Accle in 1176, and as Maior Acle and Parva Ocle in 1220, this refers to the 'woodland clearing among the oaks'. Here, the thirteenth-century records are Latin *magna* and *parva* meaning 'great' and 'small' respectively.

Locally, we find Snatchill Lodge, a name describing 'Snot's high place'.

OLD

Domesday records this name as Walda, and it is Wolde in 1291. This comes from the Old English *wald* describing the '(place at) the woodland'.

ORLINGBURY

This name is recorded as Ordlingbaere in 1066, Ordinbaro in 1086, Orlinberga in 1130, Ordelinberg in 1202, Ordinbere in 1207, Ordlingber in 1220, and Ordlingberg in 1254. Here, the origins are a Saxon personal name followed by the Old English elements *ing beorg*, giving the '(place at) the hill associated with Ordla'.

Local names include Badsaddle Lodge, a name which speaks of the '(place at) Baetti's hazel'; and Wythemail Park Farm is derived from *with mealo* or the '(place) with stones, gravel'.

ORTON

An unremarkable place name which stands out because it has no addition. Listed as Overtone in 1086 and Overton in 1263, this name comes from the Old English *uferra tun*, 'the higher farmstead' or *ofer-tun*, 'farmstead by a ridge or bank'.

OUNDLE

Information on this place name comes from as early as the eighth century. Records of Undolum in 715, Undalum and Inundalum in 730, Undala maego in 890, Undelum in

972, Undola in 1000, and Undele in 1086 show this to be from the name of the tribe which inhabited this region during and before the Roman era. Indeed, the name is quite simply from '(the settlement) of the Undalas tribe', with the tribal name thought to describe 'those without a share' or 'undivided' – which has been understood to refer to the people as shunning outsiders.

Herne Lodge was built on 'the corner of land'; indeed, it takes its name from Old English *hyrne* meaning 'corner'.

OUSE, RIVER

Although the earliest surviving records are from 1277 as Use and 1377 as Ouse, this name is undoubtedly much older. Indeed, here is a name which probably pre-dates the Celtic era, which explains why the name has never been understood.

OVERSTONE

A name which comes from a Saxon personal name followed by the Old English *tun*, telling us of 'Ufic's farmstead'. The name is recorded as Uviston in 1220 and Overston in 1236.

Chapter 15

Passenham–Pytchley

PASSENHAM

Records of this name include Passanhamm in 921 and as Passeham in 1086. These show the name comes from a Saxon personal name followed by Old English *hamm*, meaning 'the place at the river meadow of a man called Passa'.

Ashalls Copse grows by 'the spring of the ash trees'; Denshanger gets its name from 'Dynne's woodland slope'; Kings Standing Oak marks the position of a hunter's station from which to shoot game; and Puxley must have been the location for some unknown snippet of folklore, for this minor place name means 'the woodland clearing of the goblins'.

PASTON

A name which has been in Northamptonshire since recorded as Pastune in 972, although today it is considered a part of Cambridgeshire. This name comes from Old English *paesc tun*, 'the farmstead by pastureland'.

Caithwaite takes its name from the 'corner of land frequented by choughs', members of the crow family most closely related to jackdaws but which can be easily distinguished from jackdaws by brightly coloured bills and legs.

PATTISHALL

Domesday records the name as Pascelle, which by 1190 had become Pateshill. As with the previous name, this features a Saxon personal name, this time followed by *hyll*. This gives the definition of '(the place at) the hill of a man called Paetti'.

Here we find minor place names such as Astcote or 'Aefic's cottages'; Dalscote comes from 'Deorstan or Deorlaf's cottages'; Eastcote is not a compass point but from 'Eadwine's cottages'; while the Booth and Foster's Booth was originally the small hut of a poor countryman called Forster, and one which grew to become 'a fair street of inns'.

PAULERSPURY

Domesday's 1086 record of this name gives Pirie, with later listings of West Pyria, Pirye Pavely, and by 1412, Paulesperie. Unlike many other names where the manorial addition is a separate word, here it has become a single word. Originally, the settlement was from the Old English *pirige* '(place at) the pear tree'. Amazingly, although the family were here at the time of Domesday, the name of the de Pavelli family does not appear in documented records of the name until the fifteenth century. The addition was to distinguish between this place and nearby Potterspury.

Cuttle Mill is the only surviving reminder of what is now known as Ockley Brook. It does seem an odd place for a mill, for the name of Cuttle tells us it was 'intermittent', while the modern name of Ockley describes it as running through 'the woodland clearing among the oak trees'. Heathencote was once 'Heahmund's cottages'; Plumpton End was 'the farmstead where plum trees grew'; and Stockings Field is a common local name always describing the 'place marked by the tree stumps'.

The Barley Mow was an early sign showing a stack of barley, an indication that beer was brewed and sold. This must have been a very early sign, one which evolved shortly after the ale stake, the forerunner of the modern pub sign. There are many pubs named after trees; in early days, a sheaf of barley would be tied to the trunk of a tree alongside the road to show that ale was brewed nearby. By removing the lower branches and clearing away the undergrowth, this prominent tree would stand out even more.

PIDDINGTON

Listings of this name begin in 1086 with Pidentone, with later records of Pedinton in 1167 and as Pudinton in 1298. Here is a Saxon personal name followed by Old English *ing-tun*, which allows us to define the name as 'the estate associated with a man called Pyda'. It is odd to find exactly the same name and origin in neighbouring Oxfordshire, while neither name has acquired a distinguishing second element. The two are less than 25 miles apart.

The local here is the Spread Eagle, which symbolises strength and a noble bearing. For this reason, it has been adopted, not only be many families, but by a number of nations since the Romans, including the USA, Austria, Germany, Russia, Spain and France. Locally, the most likely reference is to the Montagu family.

PILTON

This name is derived from the Old English *tun* preceded by a Saxon personal name, telling us this was 'the farmstead of a man called Pileca'. It is listed as Pilchetone in 1086 and Pilkenton in 1189.

Bearshank Wood is a strange name which is an example of the way our ancestors had unusual ways of referring to everyday sights and events. Place names were intended to be recognisable; they were never names as such but descriptions of the places which would guide anyone who was travelling through unfamiliar land. This name is telling us quite literally there is 'no ham on the shank', which is a long-winded way of saying it was barren. Winning Foot Hill is a little easier to see coming from *whin* referring to 'gorse, furze'.

PIPEWELL

With listings of Pipewelle in 1086 and Pippewell in 1197, this name is not difficult to see as coming from the Old English *pipe wella* or 'the stream with the pipe, or conduit'. Whilst the name is simple to understand, the meaning may not be as simple. The most likely explanation is that the stream ran in a narrow channel, yet it is possible that the stream was artificially channelled away from its natural route, most likely for irrigation or a source of fresh water.

PITSFORD

Another Old English place name preceded by a Saxon personal name, just as so many others in Northamptonshire and elsewhere in the country. Records have been found of Pitesford in 1086, Pictesford in 1236, and Pithisford in 1270; this was 'Peoht's ford'.

PLUMPTON

Domesday records this name as Pluntune in 1086, a name from Old English *plyme tun* or 'the farmstead where plum trees grew'.

The local name of Oakley Bank is derived from *hoc leah*, 'the woodland clearing in the nook or corner of land'.

POLEBROOK

Listings of Pochebroc in 1086 and Pokebroc in 1200 are insufficient for this name to be defined conclusively. There are two potential origins, both of which have Old English origins. This is either *pohha broc*, 'the place with a pouch-shaped feature by a brook', or *pocce-broc* 'the place at the frog brook'. The former seems the most likely, as the majority of place names are coined to speak of as unique a facet as possible.

POTTERSPURY

As mentioned under Paulerspury, the basic name here is derived from Old English *pirige* meaning (the place at) the pear tree'. The addition is what it seems: it refers to the potters who worked at the pottery here and gives the place distinction from Paulerspury. It is listed as Perie in 1086, Espirie in 1239, and Potterespyrie in 1315.

Here is Wakefield Lawn, a name referring to 'Waca's *feld* or open land'.

PRESTON CAPES

There are at least thirty Prestons in England, many having a second element to make it unique, as is the case with this example. Listings of this name are found as Prestetone in 1086, Great Preston in 1256, and Preston Capes in 1335. The basic name comes from Old English *preost tun* meaning 'the farmstead of the priests' and refers to land associated with the church. The addition is manorial, a reference to the de Capes family who were here from the thirteenth century; it differentiates from the minor name here of Little Preston.

Cleaver's Clump remembers Richard Cleaver was here by 1603, while Cow Pasture Wood is not only self-explanatory but is a very common field name in Northamptonshire.

PYTCHLEY

In 956, this place was listed as Pihteslea ford, and in Domesday in 1086 as Pihteslea. Again, it is an example of a Saxon personal name followed by Old English *leah* and means 'Peoht's woodland clearing'. This is the same personal name seen at Pitsford, yet there is no reason to think this is the same person; indeed, it would be amazing if it could ever be shown that one person was indeed connected with both places.

Cox's Lodge was associated with the family of Thomas Cox of Kettering, who were here by 1635.

The local is the Overstone Arms, named from the place.

Chapter 16

Radstone–Rushton

RADSTONE

Five different records of this name have been found, as Rodestone in 1086, Rodestona in 1163, Rodestun in 1167, Rudstan in 1198, and Rodestan in 1201. Here is an Old English name from *rod stan* and meaning the '(place at) the rood stone or stone cross'. Clearly this must have been an important site, probably marking a meeting place.

Coldharbour Farm was not the most desirable location, for it described 'the exposed place'.

RAUNDS

Listed as Randun in 972, as Rande in 1086, and Raundes in 1200, this is an Old English place name which comes from a single element, *rand*, in a plural form. It tells us this was originally '(the place at) the borders or perimeter', which suggests it was adjacent to a larger estate.

Darsdale Farm gets its name from 'Deor's valley', an Old English word meaning 'deer' but here used as a personal name, while Knighton's Row remembers the family headed by George Knighton, who were here by 1650.

Raunds is known as the home of the British Army boot, and had a thriving boot and shoe industry until the 1950s. The patron saint of cobblers is St Crispin, hence the name of Crispin Way. William Nichols manufactured army boots, hence the naming of Nichols Way.

Nene Close is clearly named after the river. Webb Road is probably named after Private George Webb, who was killed in action during the First World War; he was known to all as 'Pudden' and achieved fame as the captain and centre forward for the local football team.

The George & Dragon public house shows the image of the patron saint of England and his most famous victim. While the Globe shows an image which is instantly recognisable, and also suggests the place is open to all, the name of the World Upside Down is actually a Biblical quotation from both Acts and Isaiah saying that faith will make life quite different.

Ravensthorpe welcomes us.

RAVENSTHORPE

Domesday gives this name as Ravenestorp in 1086, the only record available to us. Yet despite the lack of different forms, this can be seen as coming from a Norse personal name followed by Old Scandinavian *thorp*, which tells us it was 'Hrafn's outlying farmstead'. As with other 'outlying' names, the place would have been known as such by the community that founded it, although which place that was is unknown.

RINGSTEAD

A name found listed as Ringhestede in 1086, and as Ringstede in 1227, which points to an Old English origin of *hring stede*. The literal meaning is 'circular feature'; however, this should be understood as 'the place adjoining the circular feature'.

Originally, this was known as the Foresters Arms, later it became the Carpenters Arms, today it combines both in the tools used and is now the Axe & Compass. Nearby is the New Inn, a name which is self-explanatory, although it should probably be understood as the 'newer inn'.

The village is the birthplace of Alfred Roberts, father of former prime minister Margaret Thatcher.

ROADE

Domesday's entry of *Rode* is little different to the modern form. The name comes from the Old English *rod*, which means this began life as '(the place at) the clearing'.

The name of Hyde Farm is something of a mystery. Whilst we are clear that this is 'a hide of land', an area of land which was sufficient to support a family for a year and not exactly a measurement, for there are clearly a number of other factors to take into consideration, the mystery is that this is the only example of this name in the county when we would expect more.

ROCKINGHAM

Listings of this name begin with Domesday's Rochingeham in 1086, followed by Rogingham in 1137 and Rokingeham in 1197. This is a Saxon personal name followed by the Old English elements *inga* and *ham*, which speaks of 'the homestead of the family or followers of a man called Hroca'.

The Norman Rockingham Castle was visited by King John in the thirteenth century. He stayed here overnight the day before he lost all his baggage when attempting to cross the Wash. The King was taken ill and decided to turn back towards Wisbech, a longer but easier route, while sending his baggage train across the shorter and more difficult route along a causeway at the mouth of the Wellstream (an earlier name for the River Nene here), only crossable at the hours of the low tides. History records the tide rose rapidly and many of the horse-drawn waggons and possessions were lost, including, most significantly, the Crown Jewels.

Recent investigations by geologists have suggested the rapid tidal rise was due to a tsumani caused, as earthquakes are so rare in Britain, by an undersea mudslide. However, it is easy to backtrack and find the tide times and, knowing they would have crossed during daylight hours, find it was most likely a case of bad timing. There are also suggestions that this 'loss' was pre-arranged by John. Indeed, a twentieth-century vicar of Rockingham advised the Watson family, the owners of the property, to dig a hollow, for that was where the Crown Jewels were sure to be found.

If this was another of King John's dishonest plans, it failed, for the King's health never improved and he died at Newark-on-Trent on 19 October 1216.

ROCKINGHAM FOREST

The forest takes its name from that of Rockingham, discussed in the previous entry. Clearly, the forest was here long before the settlement, as indeed were people, thus this is not the original name for the forest. Furthermore, the extent of the woodland would have meant there would have invariably been more than one name for the forest, much as the meaning of river names shows it was pertinent to one stretch of its course and only came to the entire length when mapped and labelled. The same is probably true of Rockingham Forest; sadly none of these names have survived.

ROTHERSTHORPE

Few place names in Northamptonshire can have quite the variety of early forms as Rothersthorpe does. In 1086, it is simply Torp, by 1196, we find Trop que fuit aduocati de Bethun, in 1220, Trop Advocati, and in 1231, Retherestorp when the name becomes a little more recognisable. Here, the Old Scandinavian *thorp* is preceded by the Old English *raedere*, which tells us this was named 'outlying farm or hamlet of the councillor or advocate. The rather lengthy listing of 1196 is a reference to it being the domain of the advocate of Bethune.

The name of Arksome is derived from an Old Scandinavian personal name and Old English *hamm* and refers to 'Eirikr's hemmed in land'.

ROTHWELL

Here we find a name which means 'the stream or spring of or near the clearing'. It comes from the Old English *roth wella* and is found as Rothewelle in 1066, Ridewelle in 1086, and Rowell in 1156.

Debdale Lodge was built at 'the deep valley'; Shotwell Mill gets its name from *sceota wella* and describes 'the trout stream'; and Hospital Farm was owned by the governors of Jesus Hospital, founded in the reign of Queen Elizabeth I.

The Rothwell Charter Inn is a reminder of the charter which is celebrated each year in the Rothwell Fair. Celebrations last for a week, commencing on the day after Trinity Sunday in May or June and beginning with a procession from Holy Trinity church at six in the morning. This is traditionally led by the bailiff of the Lord of the Manor, accompanied by the local band and a guard of halberdiers – the halberd is the weapon featuring an axe on a long pole, still favoured by the Swiss Guard, who protects the Pope. This procession heads for the nearest pub and the bailiff reads the charter aloud, ending on 'God save the Queen and the Lord of the Manor', upon which the National Anthem is played and the proprietor serves the traditional rum with milk to the bailiff and his guards. The crowd cheer and then ceremoniously attempt to disarm the halberdiers – likely in the hope of receiving the free drink at every other pub in Rothwell.

The procession passes on to the Red Lion, the most common pub name in the land and heraldically referring to the Stuarts and Scotland. Locals can also enjoy a glass of their favourite tipple at the Greyhound, an old coaching inn named after the coaching service which served this 400-year-old establishment. Finally, the crowd of early risers reach their last port of call, where the owners must have deliberated for minutes before coming up with the name of The Pub.

RUSHDEN

Records have been found as Risdene in 1086, Ressendene and Rissendene in the twelfth century. This comes from the Saxon or Old English *ryscen denu* meaning 'the valley where the rushes grow'. Here is Bencroft Farm, a name which refers to 'the small field where beans are grown'.

Streets here include the themes of flowers seen in Arum Close, Yarrow Close, Meadow Sweet Road, Teasel Close, Trefoil Close, Magnolia Drive, Wisteria Close, Fuschia Way, Hyacinth Way, Crocus Way, Tulip Drive, Daffodil Drive, Campion Close, Clover Drive, Lavender Way, Foxglove Close, and Bluebell Rise. Existing names were used for Maple

Left: Needle and Awl public house at Rushden.

Below: Rushden's rather different town sign.

Wood, Hay Close, Rye Close, Greenacre Drive, and Pightles Terrace occupies a 'small enclosure of land'.

The public houses of Rushden include the invitations offered by the name of Cheers and also the Welcome Inn; both King Edward VII and the Rose & Crown show allegiance to the crown and thus the country; the Corner Flag stands on the corner, while the modern association is to a football match; that this area of England was historically greatly influenced by Norsemen is marked by the naming of the Viking; and the Needles & Awl displays these tools used by the leatherworkers, while also being a nice play on words.

RUSHTON

The similarity between this and the previous name comes from the similarity in the first element. Here, the Old English origin is *rysc tun* or 'the farmstead where the rushes grow'. This is recorded as Risetone in 1086, Riston in 1163, and Ruston in 1199.

Gaultney Wood takes its name from Old Norse *goltr* and Middle English *hey*, describing 'the enclosure where wild boars are seen'.

Rushton Hall was built of local stone in the middle of the fifteenth century by Sir John Tresham. Two centuries later, this impressive establishment was enlarged by the new owners, the Cockayne family. In 1828, the place was sold to William Williams Hope. Bought for the sum of £140,000, he spent even more money on refurbishment, even though he only put in an appearance at the hall during the shooting seasons. As holder of the office of Sheriff of Northamptonshire, he was an influential man with powerful connections, including those who gave the name to the fabulous Hope Diamond, which was said to have been found here during his time at the hall.

On the death of Hope, the hall was purchased by Miss Clara Thornhill for £165,000. A year later, in 1856, she married William Capel Clarke and the family became known as Clarke-Thornhill. Clara and Charles Dickens were very good friends, the writer staying here on a number of occasions and getting the idea for Haversham Hall from here, featured in the novel *Great Expectations*. The family are remembered by the local pub, the Thornhill Arms.

Earlier, Rushton was the birthplace of Sir Francis Tresham, the man now universally cited as the person who revealed the Gunpowder Plot to Lord Monteagle in a letter. However, the nature and content of this letter virtually confirm suspicions that Tresham and Monteagle had already spoken, thus the letter was simply confirmation of the timing of the event, thus allowing the conspirators time to make good their escape. History records all were soon captured, including Tresham, although he never faced trial, for he died inside a few days of a long-standing illness.

Chapter 17

Salcey Forest–Sywell

SALCEY FOREST

The earliest record of this name dates from 1206 as bosco de Sasceya. This comes from Old French *salceie* and Latin *salicetum* meaning 'willow'. Thus this is 'the place abounding in willows'.

SCALDWELL

Domesday's in the only record of note here, found as Scaldewelle in 1086. It comes from the Old English *scald wella*, the pronunciation being influenced by the Old Scandinavian *sk-*, and meaning '(the place at) the shallow spring or stream'.

Roseholm is an Old Norse name, nothing to do with roses but from *hross holmr* and describing 'the horse island', pointing to dry land in a marsh or seasonal wetland.

SHUTLANGER

This name is listed as Shitelhanger in 1163, Sutelhangra in 1186, and Scetelhangre in 1197. From the Old English *scytel hangra*, this has been defined as 'the wooded slope where shuttles or wooden bars are obtained'. We must assume that some family or workers made a living from managing the woodland here in order to produce growth suitable for the product(s) in which they specialised.

The local Plough Inn continues the rural theme of the local names.

SIBBERTOFT

Domesday lists this place as Sibertod, the name found as Sibertoft in 1198. Here is an Old Scandinavian name with the personal name followed by *toft*, giving 'Sigbjorn's homestead'. Alternatively, the personal name may be Saxon, in which case it would be 'Sigebeorht's homestead'.

The name of Moot Hill tells us it was 'the hill of the moot or meeting'.

Right: Slapton road sign.

Below: Silverstone village sign.

SILVERSTONE

A name synonymous with racing which began life with a very different association, which is the origin of this name. It is recorded in 942 as Sulueston, in 1086 as Selvestone, in 1130 as Seluestona, and in 1200 as Silveston. Here we find a Saxon personal name followed by Old English *tun* and meaning 'farmstead of a man called Saewulf or Sigewulf'.

Here is Olney, from *one leah* and describing 'the single or solitary woodland clearing'.

The local pub is the White Horse, which is almost certainly heraldic here. This image is found in the arms of several organisations, although here it could refer to any of the Coachmen, Wheelwrights, Saddlers, Farriers, or Innholders.

SLAPTON

Early records of this place name differ little from the modern form, even the notoriously unreliable Domesday record is as Slaptone. Undoubtedly, this is the Old English *slaep-tun*, yet the understanding depends on how the first element is used. It could be either 'the farmstead by the slippery place' or, just as likely, simply 'the muddy farmstead'. There are other Slaptons elsewhere in England and both definitions probably apply equally.

SLIPTON

The similarity between this and the previous name is not just the change of a single vowel; the meaning is virtually the same. Here we find a name from Saxon or Old English *slaep-tun*, telling us this was 'the muddy farmstead'. As with Slapton, the only record of note is in Domesday, amazingly again with an additional -e as Sliptone.

SOUTHWICK

Two common elements found in place names combine here to give a name which is found several times across the southern counties of England. Recorded as Suthwycan in 972 and Sudwic in 1130, this shows the two elements to be Old English *suth wic* or 'the southern specialised farm'. As with the vast majority of specialised farms or *wics*, the place was probably a dairy farm.

Here is Park Colsters, a place which tells us it was where charcoal makers lived and/or worked. Before coal, charcoal was an important heat source, particularly in smelting iron. Piling wood into a conical shape and then covering it in earth and turf kept out much of the oxygen and, rather than burn, the wood simply smouldered. This process removed water and impurities, thus making it burn more efficiently and producing less smoke and leaving less residue. To produce charcoal took knowledge and skill, while patience was a must, for the charcoal burners had to watch their burn for the three or more days it took to produce the product. In order to ensure they stayed awake, the burners would sit on one-legged stools, so if they slept they would fall off their seat and awaken – which is where we get the expression 'to drop off' meaning to sleep.

Other names here include Morehay Lawn or 'the enclosure near marshy ground'; Tottenhoe Lodge is from 'Totta's spur of land'; and Perio Barn and Perio Mill share an origin in 'the spur of land by the pear tree(s)'.

SPRATTON

A name listed as Spretone, Sprotone and Sprotton in the eleventh and twelfth centuries. This comes from the Old English *spreot tun*, literally 'the farmstead made from poles'. The literal meaning suggests this place was surrounded by a wooden palisade, which would have existed to keep livestock safe overnight rather than as any defensive feature.

An unsung son of Spratton is Charles Thomas Studd, who spent some thirty years as a missionary to China, India and Africa. However, he had already achieved a most notable milestone in 1882 in his earlier career as a cricketer. A right-hand batsman and quick bowler, he played in five test matches, all against Australia, including the very first international between the two nations, which has grown to become the phenomenon known as the Ashes.

STANFORD ON AVON

Found as simply Stanford in Domesday, this name comes from Old English *stan ford* and describes 'the stony ford' which enabled travellers to cross the river with a British or Celtic name meaning simply 'river'.

Here we find the name of Downtown Hill, telling us it was once the site of 'an abandoned, or depopulated former village'.

STANION

During the eleventh and twelfth centuries, there are just two listings of note, as Stanere in 1086 and Stanerna in 1163. This shows the origins to be two Old English elements, *stan* and *aern*, meaning 'the stone houses or buildings'. It has been suggested that this unusual origin may refer to a special site, maybe that of an ancient cromlech or Neolithic burial chamber. No archaeological evidence has been found, yet this is not to be unexpected considering the plough has been at work here for well over two centuries.

The Lord Nelson Inn is named after arguably England's greatest hero, a man who has had more public houses named after him than any other individual, although not always in the same way. From one of the many titles held by the Montagu family, earls of Cardigan, comes the Cardigan Arms public house.

STANWICK

Four records of this name, as Stanwige in 1086, as Stanwigga in 1125, Stanewig in 1199, and as Stanewica in 1209. The record from the early eleventh century shows the two Old English elements perfectly – *stan wigga* tells us of 'the rocking or logan stone'.

Such precariously balanced stones have endured, obviously because they have always been seen as special places. While there have doubtless been numerous examples of these being man-made, unquestionably the vast majority are natural relics of the last ice age.

Only Lord Nelson has more pubs named after him than Arthur Wellesley, who is better known by the name of the pub here, the Duke of Wellington. He had a distinguished military career in India (1797-1804), Spain and Portugal (1808-14), and the victory for which he is best remembered, at the Battle of Waterloo in 1815 when he led the forces against Napoleon Bonaparte. He later enjoyed a political career from 1819, serving as prime minister (1828-30), during which time he earned the name of the Iron Duke owing to his resilience in the face of almost universal unpopularity. Finally, he served as Foreign Secretary (1834-36) under Peel and ended his political career as Leader of the House of Lords (1841-46).

STAVERTON

Two records of note here, as Staefertun in 944 and as Stavertone in 1086. A name also found in Gloucestershire, Wiltshire and Devon, where the last county has a different origin from *staefer tun*, an Old English or Saxon name speaking of 'the farmstead made from stakes'. Clearly the inference here is to the place being surrounded by stakes. In the absence of hedgerows to define field boundaries, as is the case today, some method of keeping the livestock from wandering was necessary – hence the pallisade of stakes.

Elderstubbs Farm must have been marked by the 'stumps of elder trees'. Studborough Hill comes from *strut beorg*, an intriguing name meaning 'the hill of strife or contention' but what the dispute was is not recorded. From Old English *heort wella* or 'the stream frequented by harts' comes the name of Hartwell Spring, itself cited as the source of the River Nene.

STEANE

Found in Domesday as Stane, in 1250 as Stenes, and in 1293 as Stene, there can be no doubt this place comes from Old English *stan* or 'stone'.

Locally, we find Colready Farm, itself from an Old English term describing 'the cool stream'.

STOKE BRUERNE

As a place name, there cannot be a more common name than Stoke, which is why nearly every example has a second element; indeed, it is unusual to find such a name without the addition. The basic name comes from Old English *stoc*, which has several uses, generally defined as 'the special place' in the likelihood that the original sense is unknown. Just how the place was 'special' is rarely known; although there is the temptation to suggest some grand religious site, it is more likely to have been a storehouse or outlying secondary farmstead, possibly used only during the summer when crops were being tended or when finding alternative grazing pasture for livestock.

Listings of this name are found as Stoches in Domesday and as Stokbruer in 1254. This second record is the earliest to refer to the family who held this manor from at least the thirteenth century, namely the Briwere family.

With the Grand Union Canal running through here, we should expect to find pubs named the Boat Inn and the Navigation.

STOKE DOYLE

Listed simply as Stoche in Domesday and not as Stoke Doyle until 1428, this basic name is again 'the special place' and likely set aside for some specific purpose rather than anything spiritual.

Local names include Hatchdoyle Lane, a place where wicker hatches partitioned off 'a portion of the common field'.

STOWE NINE CHURCHES

This small parish does not have nine churches; if it did, there would be one church for every ten households. In fact, there are just two. Here the name is from Old English *stow*, which simply means 'place', although the actual meaning can be affected by other elements. Here the other elements are both correct, in the case of the two 'churches', and corrupted in the case of the number, which actually refers to the nearby River Nene.

It is worthwhile spending time examining the alternative explanations for this name, despite them mostly being examples of creative etymology. Firstly, it is claimed that from the rise of land here no less than nine individual churches can be seen. Next, the devil rears his head, blamed for having undone the hard work of the builders no less than eight times before the church was moved to a different location.

What is certain is that this was where the science of radar was developed as a practical tool for aviators.

Here is Ramsden Corner Plantation, a name referring to 'the hill where rams are reared'.

The church of St Michael contains the tomb and monument of Lady Elizabeth Carey (also known as Elizabeth Danvers, née Neville), a learned English noblewoman who had three sons and seven daughters. Her marble effigy is of the highest quality, produced by Nicholas Stone, master mason to James I, and oddly in place ten years before the death of the lady herself.

STRIXTON

This name is found as Strixton as early as 1220; the only other record is of Stricston in 1202. This is another hybrid name where an Old Scandinavian personal name precedes the Old English suffix *tun*, giving us 'farmstead of a man called Strikr'.

Note the earliest record of this name comes from the thirteenth century, suggesting this place was founded and thus named much later than most places, not during the Saxon era but around or even after the Norman conquest of England. Indeed, in the momentous year of 1066, when the Norman William arrived to claim the throne, a man named Stric is documented as holding the manor of nearby Wollaston. Furthermore, a document of 1130 cites a man working at Medehamstede as being the son of Stric. Are either of these individuals the person who gave his name to the place? If so, it would be one of the few occasions when a named man or woman is also recorded elsewhere.

SUDBOROUGH

In 1065, this name was found as Suthburhc, in 1086 as Sutburg, and in 1230 as Sudburg. This comes from two well-known Old English elements, *suth burh*, and tells us of 'the southern fortification'.

The name of Snape's Wood may have been taken as a surname but it began by describing a 'marshy place'. Visitors to the Vane Arms may reflect that this place is named after the local landowners, who were linked to the second creation of the dukes of Cleveland and barons Barnard.

SULGRAVE

This place name comes from the Old English *sulh graf* meaning 'the grove in or near a gully'. Domesday, as already noted several times in this book, is notoriously unreliable as a source of place name spellings and thus origins. However, in this case, it is the only early record available and is exactly the same as the modern form. Yet this does not cast any doubt on the definition of the name.

The history of this place goes back much further than the Washington family. Evidence exists in the names of Barrow Hill and Castle Hill, both sites of ancient earthworks.

Northamptonshire fingerpost.

Entrance to the village of Syresham.

SYRESHAM

This is a name coming from a Saxon personal name followed by the Old English element *ham*. Listed as Sigresham in 1086, as Sigeresham in 1151, and as Sigheresham in 1221, this place name began life as 'Sigehere's homestead'.

The name of Wetley's Wood is taken from 'the wheat clearing'; while Whistley Farm speaks of 'the woodland clearing in soft ground'; and Earl's Wood was held by the Earl of Leicester during the reign of Henry II (1154-89).

The locals drink in the Kings Head, the last remaining sign of the King's Brewery (1854-1954), which was based here in Broad Street. The name of the Green Man Inn is most often depicted as referring to Robin Hood and his followers, who are traditionally held to have worn clothing of Lincoln green. In truth, the name may well have referred to men wearing such attire; however, they would have been foresters rather than outlaws.

SYWELL

This name is recorded in Domesday as Siwella and as Seuewell in 1236. This name comes from the Old English *seofon wella*, meaning it is '(the place at) the seven springs'.

Chapter 18

Tansor–Twywell

TANSOR

Recorded in Domesday in 1086 as Tanesovre, this name most likely comes from the Old English *ofer* preceded by a personal name, thus meaning 'the bank or promontory of a man called Tan'. However, the first element could possibly be the Old English *tan* and used to refer to a 'branch'. If this is the case, the sense would be to refer to the same topographical feature which branched off from another.

TEETON

Found as Teche in 1086, as Teacne in 1196, and as Tekne in 1220, this name comes from Old English *taecne*, which means 'beacon'. We know that such signal sites were only constructed on the summit of hills for maximum effect. Thus the place was founded on the slopes of the 'hill with a beacon'.

THENFORD

In 1086, this name is recorded as *Taneford*, in 1130 as *Tanford*, in 1186 as *Teinford*, and in 1185 as Teneford. This name comes from the Old English *thegn ford* or 'the ford of or used by the thegns'. A thegn was a servant or retainer of a master or landholder, although just why they would be using this particular ford any more than another in order to give it such a name is unknown.

THORNBY

A name found as Torneberie in 1086, as Thirnebi in 1198, and as Turneby in 1220. This comes from the Old Scandinavian *thyrnir by*, meaning 'the village where the thorn trees grow'. As can be seen from the early forms, the suffix was originally Old English *burh*, 'fortification', but was influenced by the alternative Norse ending.

The name of Firetail Covert features a dialect name for the redstart, an insectivorous ground-feeding species, making them necessarily migrant.

THORNHAUGH

Located in a part of Northamptonshire which has been transferred to Cambridgeshire, the earliest surviving record dates from 1189 as Thornhawe. This comes from Old English *thorn haga* and describes 'the enclosure by thorn trees'.

Local names include Sibberton lodge, which began life as 'Sigeberht's *tun* or farmstead'.

THORPE MANDEVILLE

With records of Torp in 1086, Trop in 1220, and Throp Mundevill in 1306, this name undoubtedly features the Old English *throp* or 'outlying or secondary farm'. The addition shows this was held by one Richard de Amundeville by 1252, the addition being almost obligatory for such a common place name element.

The name of Magpie Farm is derived from the former Magpie public house. Contemporary customers frequent the Three Conies, named from the rabbit warrens once here, the number three only being relevant because of the sign.

THRAPSTON

Domesday lists this name as Trapestone in 1086, with later forms of Trapestona in 1138, and Thrapeston in 1285. Here is a Saxon personal name suffixed by Old English *tun*, meaning 'the farmstead of a man called Thraepst'.

Gale's Lodge was built in the region associated with the family of John Gale by 1574. Lazy Acre is a Middle English name describing poor-quality agricultural land.

Street names around the town include Roman Way, which was named because Roman artefacts were found here when the place was developed. Pashler Gardens are named after John Pashler, a former church warden whose home stood where the modern development is now seen. Clare Drive is named after poet John Clare, Sackville Street is named after the Stopford-Sackvilles, a well-known local family, as was Montagu Court after another family. Coronation Gardens was developed on land which had previously been tidied in 1953 by the Girl Guides of the town, who had planted rose bushes to mark the coronation of Queen Elizabeth II.

A relevant theme of tradesmen was given to development off Market Road, where we see Cordwainer Grove from a worker in soft leather, Wainwright Avenue is one who makes or repairs waggons, Chandlers Gardens is one associated with candles, Tyler Way is one who makes or sells tiles, Fisher Close is a trader of fish, Miller Close was a man who worked the mill, Mason Close is named after a worker in stone, Baker Court made bread, Cooper Court made barrels and kegs, and Fletchers Gardens was a man who produced arrows. A theme of castles was adopted for Windsor Drive, Warwick Gardens, Conway Drive, Arundel Close, Hever Close, Sherbourne Way, Rockingham Close, Pembroke Close, Barnwell Close, and Fotheringhay Close.

THURNING

Listed as Torninge in 1086 and Turninges in 1187, this name is also found in Norfolk and both have identical origins. Here the Old English *thyrne ing* refers to the 'place where the thorn trees grow'.

TIFFIELD

In Domesday, it was Tifelde and a century later as Tiffeld. Another name of Old English or Saxon origins in *tig feld* or 'the open land of or near the meeting place'.

The local is the George at Tiffield, most often a reference to St George, the patron saint of England, although the sign may have been changed to reflect the many years of the Georgian era.

TITCHMARSH

From the Old English personal name with *mersc* comes 'the marsh of a man called Tyccea'. It is listed as Tutean Mersc in 973, Ticceanmersc in 975, Ticemerse in 1086, and Tychemeris in 1180.

Local names here include Chequer Hill Coppice, which stands on or by the hill where the differing colours of the crops produced a chequerboard effect. Coales's Lodge was constructed where the family of Thomas and William Coles were living in 1702, while what was the self-explanatory Puddle Pit in 1779 has since been corrupted to become Polopit.

A public house named the Dog & Partridge can only be referring to the hunting of these birds for food, the man and his working dog, usually a Labrador retriever, often being depicted on the sign.

TOVE, RIVER

A river name which comes from *tof* meaning 'slow'. Although the word is rarely recorded, it is related to Middle Dutch *toeven* and Middle Low German *toven* meaning 'to linger' and will have had a root word related to both in the Germanic language family. The name is found as Toue in 1219 and as Tovebrok in 1437.

TOWCESTER

The pronunciation of a name is often a clue as to its origins, but in this case 'toaster' is quite misleading. Recorded as Tofeceaster in 921 and Tovecestre in 1086, this name means 'the Roman fort on the river Tove' with a suffix from Old English *caester*. For the river name see under its own listing.

Here we find Bury Mount, the name of a trench filled with water which has never revealed sufficient dating material to clarify when or why it was constructed. Costwell

Right: The River Tove at Towcester.

Below: A welcome to Towcester.

Farm was where vegetable matter was gathered in 'the cress spring', and Handley is a common name with several meanings but here describes 'the high woodland clearing'.

Street names here include those with a theme of birds. Here we find Linnet Road, Magpie Road, Dove Close, Nightingale Drive, Heron Close, Wren Close, and Plove Close. Trees are a popular theme, particularly when taken from, or inspired by, existing or earlier names, here represented by Woodcroft Close, Willow Close, Cedar Close, Poplar Close, Spinney Close, Oak Close, Sycamore Close, Beech Close, Holly Hill, Orchard Close, Maple Close, Juniper Close, Bramble Road, and Hazel Crescent.

Poets are remembered in another theme where we find Shelley Close, Byron Close, Tennyson Close, Keats Drive, Wordsworth Close, and Kipling Drive. Royal residences both past and present are seen by Kensington Close, Buckingham Way, Sandringham Close and Caernarvon Close. River names are seen in the street names of Broadwater Lane, Nene Lane, Brook Lane, and Ouse Lane. Plessey Close remembers the company who occupied land nearby.

Bickerstaffes Road and Sponnes Road remember Thomas Bickerstaffe, who built three almshouses here in the early nineteenth century, and his contemporary, Archdeacon Sponne, the vicar of St Lawrence, who also did much work in Towcester. The Sponne & Bickerstaffe Charity continues to benefit the needy of the town.

However, the theme derived from the nearby Silverstone racing track proved the most original idea. Hesketh Crescent remembers the Hesketh racing team, which was one of the leading manufacturers in Formula 1 during the 1970s. Tyrrel Lane recalls a Formula 1 contemporary, founded by Ken Tyrrell and which recorded thirty-three race victories. Hawthorn Drive is named after Mike Hawthorn, who won the world championship in 1958 driving for Scuderia Ferrari.

Senna Drive remembers Brazilian Ayrton Senna, who won three championships during his career, which began in 1984 and ended with a fatal crash in the 1994 San Marino Grand Prix. Lauda Way is named after the Austrian Niki Lauda, who won two championships in the first part of his career between 1971-79, ended by a near-fatal crash from which he not only recovered but returned to racing 1982-85 when he won a third title.

John Surtees, after whom Surtees Way is named, raced 1960-72 in 113 races, for eight different teams, and while he only managed six race victories, he did win the championship in 1964. However, it is his earlier career on a motorcycle for which he is more likely to be remembered. In forty-nine starts, he made the podium on all but four occasions, winning an astonishing thirty-eight of those forty-nine starts. He also won the 350cc world championship three times and 500cc version on four occasions.

Clark Crescent remembers two-time world champion Jim Clark, the Scotsman who was killed racing in a Formula 2 race in Germany in 1968. To have used just his surname would have made it difficult to discern between the father and son, hence Graham Hill Road, which recalls the father who won the championship twice in a career that spanned seventeen years from 1958, ironically killed while trying to land a Piper Aztec plane in foggy conditions.

Moss Close remembers Stirling Moss, who drove from 1951-61 winning sixteen races and yet never winning the championship owing to the dominance of Juan Manuel Fangio. Nigel Mansell, the first man to hold both Formula 1 and Indycar titles at the same time, is remembered by Mansell Close. Scotsman Eddie Irvine, who won just four of his 148 grand prix races, is remembered by Irvine Drive, while fellow countryman

David Coulthard is marked by Coulthard Close, he drove 247 grand prix races in a career covering fifteen years and amassing 535 career points, more than any other British driver.

Collins Close is a reminder of Peter Collins, a British driver who won three grand prix races in the 1950s. John Campbell-Jones gave his name to Campbell Close, this British driver drove just two races, the Belgian Grand Prix in 1962 and the British Grand Prix in 1963. The Cooper Car Company is remembered by Cooper Close, who secured two championships with their own Formula 1 cars. Brackley Road is named after the town where a number of Formula 1 construction teams have been based over the years.

Public houses of the town include the Brave Old Oak, a reminder that trees were commonly used as pointers to a pub, easy to see from some distance. Heraldic imagery gave names to the Peacock Inn, the White Hart, the White Bear, and possibly the Cock Inn. Mentioned as a stopping place for the eponymous character in Charles Dickens' *Pickwick Papers*, the landlord or owner of the Saracens Head Inn was descended from a family who took this emblem to show they had fought in the crusades. The name of the Folly Inn is something of a mystery; however, it is said to have originated from the local view that it was not the wisest of ventures – yet the thatched building is still as busy as it has ever been. However, the best name here is the Monk & Tipster, which satisfies the typical pub name by uniting two seemingly unrelated subjects. Of course, these names had to have some local basis, and while the Monk clearly refers to the church, the Tipster can only be seen by turning south-east, where we find Towcester's racecourse.

TWYWELL

All the records of this name we have come from the eleventh century and are found as Twiwel, Twiwell, Teowelle, Tviwella and Twiwell. Even today, centuries later, it is possible to recognise Old English *twi wella* as meaning '(the place at) the double spring or stream'.

Dr David Livingstone, missionary and explorer, had two faithful companions named Chuma and Susi. After his death, they brought pieces of the bark body carrier back with them to the church, while they took up residence in the church rectory.

Chapter 19

Wadenhoe–Wootton

WADENHOE

Listed in Domesday as Wadenho in 1086 and in 1186 as Wadeho, this name comes from the Old English *hoh* preceded by a Saxon personal name. During the pre-Norman era, this place was founded as '(the place at) the hill spur of a man called Wada'.

WAKERLEY

A name found in Domesday as Wacherlei and as Wakerle in 1209. There are two equally plausible Old English origins for this name. Either this is *wacor feld*, giving 'the woodland clearing of the watchful ones', or *wacra feld*, which would describe 'the woodland clearing where osiers grow'. If the former is the case, it would not be as sinister as the literal meaning would seem, simply that the place was guarded, although this does lead to the obvious question of why but this will never be known.

WALGRAVE

First seen in Domesday as Waldgrave and in 1202 as Waldegrave, this name comes from the Old English or Saxon element *graf* meaning 'grove'. The first element is certainly *wald*, 'wood', but this is likely the original name and here the name comes from the place name of Old and therefore 'the grove belonging to Old' should be given as the definition.

Amber Drive, cut alongside the playing fields, takes the name of the local football team, Walgrave Amber.

WAPPENHAM

Early records are all very similar to Domesaday's Wapeham. The name comes from Saxon personal name suffixed by Old English *ham* and meaning 'Waeppa's homestead'.

The name of Blackmire's Farm is taken from its 'dark pool'; Cockerell's Copse reminds us that Elizabeth Cockrill was here by 1716; and Potash is named from the former Potash Farm, here in 1826 and where, somewhat predictably, potash was produced.

WARKTON

A name from Old English *ing tun* which follows the personal name seen in the definition 'the estate associated with Weorca'. It is recorded several times in the eleventh, twelfth and thirteenth centuries as Werkentune, Werchintone, Werketon, Wercheton, and Werkinton.

WARKWORTH

A name recorded as Wauercuurt in 1153, as Wavercurt in 1208, and as Wauerheworthe in 1220. This comes from Old English *laewerce leah* or 'the woodland clearing where larks are seen'.

  Franlow Knob Farm is from 'Franca's mound or tumulus'; Grimsbury tells us it was 'Grim's fortification'; and Huscote House was built on what was formerly 'Hussa's cottages'.

WARMINGTON

Recorded in 980 as Wyrmingtun and in 1086 as Wermintone, here is an Old English *ing tun* preceded by a Saxon personal name. This place began life as 'the estate associated with a man called Wyrma'.

  Eaglethorpe is from 'Ecgwulf's *thorp* or outlying farmstead', while what was 'Pappa's woodland clearing' is today marked on the map as Papley.

WATFORD

This name is recorded in Domesday as in the modern form. It comes from the Old English *wath ford*, meaning 'the ford used when hunting'.

  Silsworth Lodge takes the name of the place which existed here well before it was built; it is derived from 'Sifel's *worth* or enclosure'. Burnham's Barn is the sole reminder of the family of Richard Burnham, who are first recorded here in 1603.

WATLING STREET

One of the longest roads in the country and yet it is named from those at one small part of it. In 944, this name is found as Waeclinga straet. This name refers to the British tribe who lived around that part of the road south of St Albans (known to the Romans as Verulaneum), hence the 'road associated with the Waecling'. Here the name is thought to refer to 'the people of or associated with a man called Wacol'.

WEEDON LOIS

Records of this name include Wedone in 1086, Leyes Weedon in 1475, and Loyeswedon in 1535. This is a name seen in several places, which always tells us of *weoh dun* or 'the hill with a heathen temple'. Because of more than one in the county, there is an affix. Here, the origins of the addition are uncertain, being given as possibly the Christian name of a family who were lords of the manor, or possibly a well dedicated to St Lewis or St Loys. However, documented evidence is lacking to support either theory.

The Plume of Feathers public house features the sign which was first adopted as symbolising the Black Prince. Son of Edward III and father to Richard II, he died a year before his father and thus became the first Prince of Wales not to inherit the throne. The Weedon Bec pub reminds us of a minor stream, while the Narrow Boat Inn refers to the nearby Grand Union Canal.

WEEKLEY

In 956, we find this name as Wicleaford, in 1086 as Wiclei, in 1094 Wichelai, in 1167 Wichelea, and in 1199 as Wicle. This unites the two Old English elements *wic* and *leah*. The latter refers to a woodland clearing, but the former is normally only seen as a suffix and meaning 'specialised farm' and nearly always thought to be a dairy farm. However, here this is not the case and therefore it must be an alternative specialised settlement or have a different origin. This may be Old English *wice* referring to the wych elm, although for this to be the case, there would have to have been a substantial number of these trees – indeed, more than are normally found occurring naturally.

Boughton House is an unusual corruption from Old English *boc tun*, which describes 'the farmstead among the beech trees'.

WELDON (GREAT AND LITTLE)

Records of Parva Weledene and Walesdone in Domesday, Welledon in 1163, and Magna Welledon in 1186 show this to be from Old English *wiella dun*, 'the hill with a spring or stream'.

Bangrave Wood tells us it was 'the barn by a woodland grove', while Cowthick Lodge was built on the land named after 'the thicket by the cows'.

The Woolpack takes the name of the 240-pound bale which was the standard packaging for the raw material of the wool trade. The Shoulder of Mutton is often taken from the name given to the topography of the land, others may refer to the landlord also performing the role of the local butcher, and it was also a staple offering at inns in former times.

WELFORD

Here is a name from Old English *wella ford* or 'the ford by the spring'. The element *wella* is also used to mean 'stream'; however, this does not seem likely here, for all fords cross such a feature and place names are rarely so general. The name is found as Wellesford in Domesday.

The names of both the Hemploe and Hemplow Hills have identical origins in Old English *hinda plaga* or 'the place where hinds play'.

The Wharf Inn is located on a short arm of the Grand Union Canal.

WELLAND, RIVER

Records of Weolud in 921, Ueuolod in 1000, and Weiland in 1106 show this to be of Celtic or British origins. As already stated elsewhere in this book, the Celtic tongue had no written form and we can only define the terms by association with related languages such as Welsh, Cornish, Irish, and Breton. The modern name has undoubtedly been influenced by the Saxons and *wella* and *land*, although there is no link to these Old English terms.

This is related to Celtic *vesu* 'good', or Welsh *gwiw* 'fitting', and Latin *dignus* also 'fitting', while the second element may be likened to Old Irish *luaid* 'to move'. Thus, perhaps this was simply 'the good river' and describing the quality of its water.

The embankment alongside the River Nene at Wellingborough.

WELLINGBOROUGH

Whether this place is found as Wendlesberie as in 1086, or Wenlingeburg in 1199, or as Wendlingburgh in 1220, the origin is undoubtedly a Saxon personal name followed by *inga burh*. Thus here we have an origin of 'the fortification of the family or followers of Waendel'.

Appleby Gate is derived from the family, who take their surname from the place in Leicestershire, who were lords of the manor from 1292, when Henry de Appleby held this place. Croyland Hall Farm is also manorial, referring to this being a possession of the Abbot of Croyland by 1199.

Pubs here include the Crown & Anchor. The symbol of the Lord High Admiral and worn on the sleeve of all petty officers in the Royal Navy, it is a favourite of retired officers who return to land as publicans.

The days when public houses were the equivalent of motorway service stations are commemorated by names such as Coach & Horses, Nags Head, Horseshoe Inn, and the Gloster, which was a famous coaching service. Later came the railways and a new source of inspiration for names such as the Locomotive. Local landmarks are always popular, for they can act as signposts to the pub. Here we find examples such as the Litten Tree, Cottage Inn, Priory, Park Tavern,

The nobility are represented by the Royal, Prince of Wales, Queens Head, and the Duke of York of nursery rhyme fame. The duke in question is Frederick Augustus (1763-1827), son of George III, who commanded the English army in Flanders. However, the rhyme does the man no favours, for while he may well have been 'Grand', he certainly was not old, for he was only thirty-one at the time. Neither did he lead 10,000 men up or down hills, for there are no hills around here and he had a minimum of 30,000 men under his command. Patriotic names include the British Arms and the George Inn, after the patron saint.

Heraldry is always a popular theme; the image seen outside the Cannon could refer to any of the children of Henry VIII who ascended to the throne after him, Edward VI, Queen Mary, or Queen Elizabeth I. The Star Inn is a religious symbol: often portrayed as the star of Bethlehem, it also refers to the Virgin Mary. The Eagle has been used to represent more families than any other image; the Golden Lion represents either Henry I or the Percy family, dukes of Northumberland; the Ranelagh Arms after that Irish peerage; and the Vivian Arms comes from the barons Vivian.

The Boot Inn is named to remember the old boot factory, a major local employer for many years. This industry is also the reason for the Crispin Arms, St Crispin being the patron saint of boot makers. The Volunteer is named for the soldiers who offered their services in the two world wars and the Napoleonic wars. The Hind Hotel is the former home of Sir Christopher Hatton, lord of this manor. He was a sponsor of Sir Francis Drake on his voyages, Drake naming one of his ships the *Golden Hind* from the heraldic symbol on the family crest, a vessel which had left on the first circumnavigation of the globe as the *Pelican* and was renamed during the voyage.

The Red Well, which differs from the place name of Redwell, is named after the 'reedy spring' where King Charles I brought his nineteen-year-old consort, Queen Henrietta Maria, in 1628. To partake of these waters was said to be be an excellent remedy for fertility problems. Whether they are or not is unrecorded, yet by the time they returned nine years later they had had four children. The Dog & Duck is another with royal connections, for Charles II in particular was fond of this hunting method, where ducks with clipped wings were released on to a local pond. Unable to escape by flight, they would attempt to avoid the dogs by diving. In later years, the name is often interpreted as the more easily recognised modern duck hunter with his faithful retriever.

The Ock 'n' Dough is a pub name chosen from suggestions by locals. Just after the Millennium celebrations had ended, the new pub was open and named for a traditional local delicacy. This consists of a pork hock (or 'Ock) with potatoes in a vegetable stock which, when baked in a pie, produces a soft pastry (or 'Dough') base and a crisp top crust. While a change of owner means the pie is sadly no longer on sale here, it is still savoured by the community.

Street names include that of Winstanley Road named after Gerrard Winstanley, the founder of the so-called Diggers, an agrarian community of the mid-seventeenth century whose history is hardly recorded, which suggests this was deliberate, while the street name comes from public knowledge. Furthermore, the names of neighbouring streets suggest the name was probably chosen to commemorate some (unknown) act by Winstanley. Here, Knox Road and Newcomen Road are named after John Knox, the Scottish Presbyterian clergyman, and Matthew Newcomen, an English nonconformist preacher. Ranelagh Road takes its name from the pub, itself from the Irish peerage; the earls Spencer, based at Althrop, gave their name to Spencer Road; and Palk Road, is named after Sir Robert Palk, cleric and politician.

Other streets have themes, golf being the basis for the names of Hoylake, Muirfield Road, Wentworth Avenue, Troon Crescent, and Gleneagles Drive. The Lake District provided the inspiration for the names which include: Coniston Drive, a town, a lake known as Coniston Water, and the fell known as the Old Man of Coniston; Penrith Drive is after the popular market town; Windermere Drive is named after the town (known as Birthwaite prior to the arrival of the railway) and the largest lake in England; Bowness is a road named after the town which stands on Lake Windermere and is officially known as Bowness-on-Windermere, the town of Windermere itself being about a mile up the hill; and Thirlmere Drive is named after the two lakes, Leathes Water and Wythburn Water, which were dammed to create a reservoir to feed the city of Manchester in the 1890s.

There is also an avian theme, featuring Nest Farm Crescent, Nest Lane, Fulmar Lane, Gannet Lane, Kestrel Lane, Linnet Close, Heron Close, Guillemot Lane, Sandpiper Lane, Robin Lane, Osprey Lane, Swallow Lane, and Thrush Lane.

WELTON

Records of this name include Walteden in 1198, Waltendun in 1204, and Welteden in 1248. This is probably derived from an Old English stream name from *wealt*, meaning 'shaky, unsteady, rolling', here with the additional *denu* and thus 'the rolling stream of the valley'.

Minor names here include Churchill House, built on the place which was known for its 'hill with a church'. Hobberhill Farm takes the place name from Old English *holh beorg hyll*, which describes 'the hollow hill, hill'. From *micel wielle* or 'the big spring' comes Mickle Well, a water source described as emerging from a fissure four inches deep and twelve wide.

The Clarke family built Welton Place for themselves in 1758 and held it for over a century. A reminder of their influence is seen in the form of Clarkes Way.

WERRINGTON

Found as Witheringtun in 972 and as Widerintone in Domesday, this place was always a part of Northamptonshire until the change in county boundaries in 1974. This features a Saxon personal name and Old English *ing tun* and describes 'the farmstead associated with a man called Wither'.

Locally is Hamfield Farm, a term which suggests this was 'low-lying pasture'.

WEST HADDON

Recorded as Westhaddon in 1220, this name has its addition to differentiate from East Haddon. The basic name comes from the Old English *haeth dun* or 'the hill of the heath or heather'.

The houses in Elizabeth Road were built in 1953, the year of the coronation of Elizabeth II, while off here is Victoria Close, thus carrying on the theme of female monarchs. Lattimore Close remembers Mr Lattimore, headmaster of West Haddon Primary School for thirty-four years from 1936. Doctor Morrison was an important member of the community during his long life and well merits the naming of Morrison Park Road in his honour. Mr Parnell gave his name to Parnell Close.

There really was a forge in Old Forge Drive; indeed, it was still here until 1960. Atterbury Close recalls the influential family who lived at Manor Farm from 1848; the land has since been developed but signs of the past are everywhere in names such as Field Close and Dairy Close.

However, surely the most deserved street name in the village is that of Muncaster Way. Widowed in her native Shropshire, she first moved to Winwick with her son, but when the brook burst its banks and her house flooded, Nurse Muncaster was assisted by the nursing committee and she was housed in West Haddon. Her area of responsibility also covered Yelvertoft, Clay Coton, Crick and Lilbourne, besides West Haddon and Winwick. She arrived in the village shortly after 1940, staying until her death in 1991 at the age of eighty-six, just nine years after she had given up working. During the four decades, she brought an astonishing number of babies into the world; indeed, an entire generation emerged into her hands, for, as several doctors noted, all were pushed aside when Nurse Muncaster arrived at a confinement.

Other names here include Ostor Hill, a name from Old Scandinavian *austr haugr* and describing 'the eastern barrow or burial mound'.

WESTON FLAVELL

With a record of Weston in Domesday, this is 'the western farmstead'. Clearly, this is a common place name and the addition is expected. Here it is manorial reference to Johannes Fauvel who was here in 1232; here, the surname is thought to be a nickname from Old French *fauvel* meaning 'fallow-coloured'.

Locally is the name of Booth Farm which can have one of two meanings. If this is a dialect word, then booth means 'cowhouse', or if it is Old Norse *both*, then it refers to a 'temporary enclosure'.

Public houses here include the delightfully named Clicker, a term from the local shoe-making industry. This name was given to the foreman who allotted cut pieces of leather to the workforce. The Bold Dragoon refers to the solider who carried a carbine, a short form of musket. This shortened barrel made firing it resemble the fire-breathing dragon, a corruption of which gave the soliders the name Dragoons.

WHILTON

Recorded as Woltone in 1086, Whelton in 1200, and Hwelton in 1254, this name comes from Old English *hweol tun* and describes 'the farmstead by the round hill'.

WHILTON BROOK

A name recorded as Wheltonbroc in the thirteenth century, this name is an example of back formation – that is, derived from a place name, that of Whilton, which is defined under its own entry.

WHITTLEBURY

Records of Witlanbyrig in 930 and Wytlebyr in 1316, this name tells us of 'Witla's fortification'.

Local names include Cattle Hill Wood, which has been suggested to be 'wild cat spring' but more likely this first element is the male personal name Cat; the Gullet describes the shallow depression in which a stream flows; while Chamber's Sale Copse refers to the name of Adam de la Chaumbre, who was here by 1275, with Sale either from *sealh* or 'willow trees' or a dialect word for a division of land.

The Fox & Hounds public house is a reminder of the days when pubs would have been the focal or meeting point for the hunt, or maybe the landlord was also the kennel master.

WHITTLEWOOD FOREST

A name which is found as Whitlewuda in 1383. This is not the first name for this forest, for it existed before the settlement of Whittlebury from which the name is derived.

WICKEN

Recorded as Wicha in 1086, as Wikes in 1209, and as Wyca Mainfein in 1254, this name comes from *wicum* or 'the specialised farms'.

Here is Dagnall, a local place name describing 'Dagga's nook of land'.

WILBARSTON

Seen in Domesday as Wiberdestone, in 1156 as Wilbertestun, and in 1157 as Wilberdestun, here is a name featuring Old English *tun* and a Saxon personal name and speaking of 'Wilbeorht's farmstead'.

Askershaw Wood is derived from 'Askertill's enclosure'; Barrowdykes Wood is from *bearu dic* or 'the ditches in the woodland'; and what began as 'Pippa's spring' is now known as Pipewell.

WILLOW BROOK

This tributary of the Nene is recorded as the Willowbrook in 1791, a name which is self-explanatory in stating that willow trees abound upon its banks. This late record suggests this was not the original name, and yet this will remain unknown, for there are no records which can be related to this water course.

WITTERING

Now a part of Cambridgeshire but, until the late twentieth century, a part of Northamptonshire. Records such as Witheringaeige in 972, as Witheringham in 1086, and as Witeringa in 1167 show this to be from a Saxon personal name and Old English *inga eg* and thus 'the island of the family or followers of a man called Wither'.

Here the name of Bonemills Farm tells us it was 'the mill for crushing or grinding bones', animal bones used as a fertiliser.

WOLLASTON

A name found as Wilavestone in 1086 and as Wullaueston in 1190, this name features a Saxon personal name and Old English *tun* and thus refers to 'the farmstead of a man called Wulflaf'.

WOODEND

A very common minor place name which is most often found as two words; however, the meaning is the same in both cases. The name comes from the Old English *wudu ende*, meaning '(the place at) the edge of the wood'. The earliest record of this name comes from 1316 as Wodende.

Kirby Grounds was once known as 'Kaeri's *by* or village', while War's Farm has nothing to do with armed conflict but comes from Robert War of Sulgrave, who was associated with this place by 1631; and the name of Cathanger Farm may indeed speak of 'wild cat slope' but is more likely to be a personal name, as in 'Cat's slope'.

Above left: The Coronation Clock marks the crowning of Queen Elizabeth II in 1953, on the side of the Wollaston Inn.

Above right: Wollaston's village sign shows the importance of shoe making in the county.

Right: Wollaston signpost.

WOODFORD

It would seem this name is still as obvious in meaning today as it was when it was coined well over a thousand years ago. Indeed, it is still recognisable in Domesday as Wodeford and is from the Old English *wudu ford* describing the 'ford in or by a wood'.

Minor names here include West Farndon, 'the western hill where ferns grow'; Hinton is from *higna tun* or 'the farmstead of a religious community'; and Warden Grange takes the name of 'the monks of Warden Abbey', which is found in neighbouring Bedfordshire and who once held this land.

The church, known as the Cathedral of the Nene, has a glass case containing a human heart. It is said to have belonged to Lord Trailly and brought back here after he was killed fighting in the Crusades.

The local pubs include the Dukes Arms, which refers to the local family of the Arbuthnots and, in particular, Charles Arbuthnot, who was Chancellor of the Duchy of Lancaster (1828-30). Woodford House, the Arbuthnot home, is a nineteenth-century mansion which is probably best known for being where the diarist Harriet Arbuthnot died in 1833. Harriet was as close to the British aristocracy as it is possible to be, was a long-time friend and correspondent of the Duke of Wellington, and was party to just about every political decision and personal detail of the establishment in the early nineteenth century. Harriet Arbuthnot's life was brought to a sudden end in 1834 after she contracted cholera.

WOODFORD HALSE

As with the previous name, this is 'the ford in or by a wood'. The name is recorded as Wudeford in 1224, the name getting its addition from the manor of Halse here.

WOODNEWTON

This name was recorded in Domesday as simply Niwetone and in 1255 as *Wodenneuton*. The basic name here comes from Old English *niwe tun* meaning 'the new farmstead', with the later addition of *wudu* 'at the wood'.

WOOTTON

A common place name normally found with a distinctive addition. Here, the basic name is found as Witone in 1086 and Wotton in 1202. This is from Old English *wudu tun* or 'the farmstead in or near the wood'.

The Yeoman of England public house takes its name from either the foot soldiers or possibly the yeoman farmers.

Chapter 20

Yardley Gobion–Yelvertoft

YARDLEY GOBION

Recorded as Gerdeslai in 1160, Jerdelai in 1167, and Yerdele Gobioun in 1353, the basic name is a common one and comes from the Old English *gyrd leah*. This tells us it was 'the wood where rods or spars were obtained'. With common place names additions are to be expected and here it is manorial, a reference to the Gubuyn family, who were here by the thirteenth century.

One local name of note is Queen's Oak, said to be where the then Edward of York, later Edward IV, first met Elizabeth Woodville. Her children included Queen Elizabeth, consort of Henry VII, and Edward V, grandchildren included Prince Arthur, who died before he ascended to the throne and thus Henry VIII was crowned, and later generations included members of the Stuart, Hanover and Windsor families who ruled not only England but Scotland, France, Germany, Ireland and India too.

In the eighteenth century, coffee houses were popular meeting places. It seems that a number of pubs took the name to promote themselves as alternative venues, hence the name of the Coffee Pot which, we can only assume, must have sold cups of coffee too.

YARDLEY HASTINGS

Another name from *gyrd leah*, 'the wood where rods or spars were obtained'. Here, the addition is, like the previous name, manorial and refers to the de Hastinges family, who were here by the thirteenth century, as evidenced by the record of Yerdele Hastings in 1316.

Local names include Arniss Copse or 'the eagle's spur of land'; Blenley Lodge describes 'the hidden or blind woodland clearing'; Grimpsey Copse was 'Grim's *leah* or woodland clearing'; Cowper's Oak is named after the poet William Cowper, who is said to have frequented this place; and Gog Oak and Magog Oak are named after the Biblical giants and chosen for they are somewhat larger than Cowper's Oak.

YARWELL

Listed as *Jarwelle* in 1166, this name comes from the Old English *gear wella*, meaning 'the spring by the dams for catching fish'. Here is the kind of name which the author is delighted to find, for it gives an instant image of life during the Saxon era: the image of the poles across the stream with wickerwork baskets tied between and used to trap the fish of the minimum required size.

YELVERTOFT

Domesday lists this place as *Gelvrecote*, which by the twelfth century had become *Gelvertoft*. These forms have made definition difficult to tie down. One idea is that it is from a Saxon personal name with the addition of Old Scandinavian *toft*, although the Domesday record shows the earlier *cot* 'cottage', which would give a meaning of 'Geldfrith's homestead'. Alternatively, the first part of the name may be Old English *geol ford* with *toft*, which would produce 'the homestead of the ford by the pool'. Unless other forms are found, the name is likely to remain undefined.

Speller Farm is thought to be derived from 'speech hill', for while written evidence is inconclusive, this is a long hill and this is a place where many old roads and footpaths converge, itself a strong indication of this being an important meeting place.

Common Place Name Elements

ELEMENT	ORIGIN	MEANING
ac	Old English	oak tree
banke	Old Scandinavian	bank, hill slope
bearu	Old English	grove, wood
bekkr	Old Scandinavian	stream
berg	Old Scandinavian	hill
birce	Old English	birch tree
brad	Old English	broad
broc	Old English	brook, stream
brycg	Old English	bridge
burh	Old English	fortified place
burna	Old English	stream
by	Old Scandinavian	farmstead
ceap	Old English	market
ceaster	Old English	Roman stronghold
cirice	Old English	church
clif	Old English	cliff, slope
cocc	Old English	woodcock
cot	Old English	cottage
cumb	Old English	valley
cweorn	Old English	quern
cyning	Old English	king
dael	Old English	valley
dalr	Old Scandinavian	valley
denu	Old English	valley
draeg	Old English	portage
dun	Old English	hill
ea	Old English	river
east	Old English	east
ecg	Old English	edge
eg	Old English	island
eorl	Old English	nobleman
eowestre	Old English	fold for sheep
fald	Old English	animal enclosure
feld	Old English	open land
ford	Old English	river crossing

ELEMENT	ORIGIN	MEANING
ful	Old English	foul, dirty
geard	Old English	yard
geat	Old English	gap, pass
haeg	Old English	enclosure
haeth	Old English	heath
haga	Old English	hedged enclosure
halh	Old English	nook of land
ham	Old English	homestead
hamm	Old English	river meadow
heah	Old English	high, chief
hlaw	Old English	tumulus, mound
hoh	Old English	hill spur
hop	Old English	enclosed valley
hrycg	Old English	ridge
hwaete	Old English	wheat
hwit	Old English	white
hyll	Old English	hill
lacu	Old English	streamlet, water course
lang	Old English	long
langr	Old Scandinavian	long
leah	Old English	woodland clearing
lytel	Old English	little
meos	Old English	moss
mere	Old English	lake
middel	Old English	middle
mor	Old English	moorland
myln	Old English	mill
niwe	Old English	new
north	Old English	north
ofer	Old English	bank, ridge
penn	Old English	rocky hill
pol	Old English	pool, pond
preost	Old English	priest
ruh	Old English	rough
salh	Old English	willow
sceaga	Old English	small wood, copse
sceap	Old English	sheep
stan	Old English	stone, boundary stone
steinn	Old Scandinavian	stone, boundary stone
stapol	Old English	post, pillar
stoc	Old English	secondary or special settlement
stocc	Old English	stump, log
stow	Old English	assembly or holy place
straet	Old English	Roman road
suth	Old English	south

ELEMENT	ORIGIN	MEANING
torr	Old English	rock hill or outcrop
thorp	Old Scandinavian	outlying farmstead
treow	Old English	tree, post
tun	Old English	farmstead
wald	Old English	woodland, forest
wella	Old English	spring, stream
west	Old English	west
wic	Old English	specialised, usually dairy farm
withig	Old English	willow tree
worth	Old English	an enclosure
wudu	Old English	wood

Bibliography

Oxford Dictionary of English Place Names by A. D. Mills
Concise Oxford Dictionary of English Place Names by Eilert Ekwall
A Dictionary of Pub Names by Leslie Dunkling and Gordon Wright
Chronicle and Echo
Street Names by Thrapston Town Council
Streets of Character: A Stroll through the Streets of West Haddon by West Haddon Local History Group
Aynho: A Northamptonshire Village by Nicholas Cooper
Lost and Hidden Kettering by Kettering Civic Society
Northamptonshire Place Names by Charles Whynne-Hammond
The Place Names of Northamptonshire by J. E. B. Gover
The Street Names of Burton Latimer by John Meads
Long Buckby at the Millennium by Long Buckby Local History Society